CHARMAIN JARRETT

Prophetic Fasting

Touching the heart of God through Fasting

*This book is dedicated to
my family who believe in me and the vision that God has given me.
And to all the partners of Jesus Strong Ministries.*

*"Let your roots grow down into him, and let your lives be built on him.
Then your faith will grow strong in the truth you were taught, and you will
overflow with thankfulness." Colossians 2:27*

Contents

Acknowledgement

I wish to express gratitude and heartfelt thank you to the intercessors who prayed with me for the birth of this book. They are the reason this book is a reality;

To Ms. Rebecca Mumby for living a life of fasting and prayer.

To Niasha Hawkins for her wholehearted, sincere desire to fan the flame.

To Denotra Robbins for her insatiable thirst for the word of God.

To my wonderful husband, Mervin Jarrett, who sacrificed so much so that God could use me.

To my dear children; Romaine, Shannon, Jordan, and Jayden, for understanding when mom was unavailable.

Thank you to all the partners of Jesus Strong Ministries.

Preface

During a "Her Voice" women's conference in Portland, Oregon, Lou Engle's inspirational message on fasting captivated my attention. As I listened intently, I saw a vision of many pregnant women ready for birth but lacking the strength to deliver. Several of them were waddling around, unaware that they were about to give birth. I also saw others who were about six months pregnant or less. As I pondered the scene in my mind's eye, the term "pregnant midwife" popped into my mind. I thought those who are less far along in their pregnancy, will need to assist those who are ready to give birth.

My body suddenly felt weighted down, and I literally doubled over in my chair under the pressure. The pressure was so great that it broke my genuine leather belt. The Lord asks, "Will you help Me birth My next move on the earth?" Although I was not sure what He meant, I said, "Yes." The conference was all about giving our "*yes*" to God.

In the days leading up to the conference, I was finishing up this book but got stuck in one of the chapters. It seemed as if the Lord was telling me to wait until after the conference to complete it. I did not know what the speakers were going to talk about or that it would have anything to do with the book.

Although I was obedient to write the book, I was thinking there are already many books on fasting, so why write another? Lou Engle prophesied during the conference that, "a Jesus fast was going to precede a Jesus movement." As Lou Engle continued to speak, the anointing intensified until I felt like I was about to burst. It became apparent to me that this book on fasting will give those pregnant women the strength to deliver their spiritual babies. As I pondered the vision I became aware that the women in my vision were pregnant with revival.

When I returned home from the conference and I literally felt a fire in me driving me to complete the book. So if you are holding this book, you might be pregnant with a mighty move of God. And no, you don't have to be a woman to be pregnant with Revival. God is looking for people that will tap into the power of prophetic fasting and birth a global revival in this generation.

Fasting Experiences

Fasting has always been an integral part of my life. In fact, I started fasting when I was ten years old. I didn't understand what it meant, but I did it because I saw adults doing it. Throughout my life, I frequently practiced fasting. I fasted for forty days before deciding to marry my husband. I fasted when I first gave my life to Jesus and when He called me into ministry and I frequently fast and pray for my family and for God's direction.

The Lord led me to call a corporate fast for twenty-one days, but there was something different about this fast. We did not have any dire circumstances or judgment pronounced upon us; the Holy Spirit simply led us to fast, and we obeyed.

A group of us prayed together every morning of the twenty-one-day fast over a conference call. During the fast, we repented and prayed for ourselves and on behalf of our families, nation, and believers everywhere. Each morning, The Holy Spirit led us to pray for different situations within our families, the church, and in the world.

Two days before commencing the fast, the Holy Spirit inspired me to call it, "Heart of God Fasting" because I felt as though God was inviting us to explore His heart. This was not your regular fasting for a breakthrough or for protection, it wasn't about coming to God with a need, it was all about learning what was in His heart.

Prophetic Fasting

Then The Lord directed me to write a brief email summarizing the lessons we discussed each day. It moved my heart to hear the testimonies of those who read the emails but could not participate in the fast. As I read the testimonies, The Lord instructed me to collect all twenty-one emails and publish them in a book. While writing the book, God revealed the connection between fasting and the prophetic. Then he instructed me to title the book Prophetic Fasting: Touching the Heart of God Through Fasting. Almost every fast in the Bible is preceded by some prophetic word or results in some prophetic utterance. God is calling people back to prophetic fasting because it is the only way to touch God's heart and bring His kingdom to Earth. Many prophecies are yet to be fulfilled, and God is looking for people who understand the times we live in and fast and pray until they are fulfilled.

During our ministry's twenty-one-day fast, The Lord repeatedly highlighted Psalm 122:1-2. *I was glad when they said to me, "Let us go into the house of the Lord." Our feet have been standing within your gates, O Jerusalem!* In some cultures, it is common for people to visit each other but not enter their homes until invited in. The visitor would stand at the door until the owner invited them in. It is also customary for guests to take off their shoes or wash their feet before entering the home, depending on their culture. Washing feet is common in cultures where people wear sandals or walk barefoot.

Like the Psalmist, we felt as if we were standing inside the gates of the Lord's courtyard, at His doorway, but He invited us to come inside His house for a twenty-one-day journey of exploring His heart. As we began the fast, The Lord revealed the hidden things in our hearts through visions, revelations, and prophecies, word of knowledge, and allowed us to experience His heart for humanity. Many people confessed their sins, repented, and received healing and breakthroughs. It was a great pleasure for us to receive this divine invitation and to experience the Heart of God through fasting.

Waiting at the Door

One participant received a vision from the Lord on the second day of the fast. She described a vision of many people walking up a staircase that stretched from earth into heaven, similar to Jacob's dream. Eventually, they reached a threshold in the sky but could not pass it. There was a door with more stairs behind it, but no one could get past the door. A group of angels stood to the right of the people and explained that they need to be washed before they could go any further. The people agreed to be washed, but the angels told them they could not cleanse themselves. In this vision, many people were kneeling in prayer. The people at the threshold had to wait until they were all washed before entering through the doors.

Every morning during the fasting prayer, the lady said she would go to the same place in her vision, and she would see the people waiting to be washed. On the twentieth day of fasting, she said, there was a difference. The angel was not there, and the people were kneeling in a praise position, with their hands lifted. On the twenty-first day of the fast, there was no angel, and the door was wide open, and the glory of The Lord's presence shined through it like, beautiful, brilliant sunlight, and the people entered the glorious presence of The Lord. They made their way down another stairway that resembled a movie theater, and the steps were the same width on the way down as they were on the way up. It was a glorious place and each person could feel the brilliance of the presence of God saturating their souls. As the people walked in order step by step, they praised and thanked God for allowing them to enter His glorious presence. God wants people to know that if they choose to be washed in the blood of Jesus, their sins are forgiven and they are free to enter His glorious presence.

While you journey through your allotted days of fasting, humble yourself and allow Him to wash you, and you will encounter the Lord's Holy presence. When you allow God to cleanse you, He will reveal things in your heart that you do not want to hear or see. As He reveals these hidden things in your heart, you may feel tempted to deny them, but you cannot enter God's presence until He cleanses you. Therefore, accept what He reveals to you and repent from it. Our 21-Day fasting resulted in many confessions of sin, which led to inner healing and deliverance, and peace with God.

Prior to starting your fast, let's take care of a few fasting housekeeping items so that you can have a successful fast. People sometimes asked, What is fasting? Why is it necessary? When should we fast and how should we fast? I will attempt to answer those questions before you fast so that you can fast with the proper perspective.

Pre-Fasting

The Origin of Fasting

Fasting originated in the days of Moses; although it could be prior to this; he was the first person to mention fasting in Exodus 34:28 when he was on the mountain with the LORD for forty days and forty nights without eating bread or drinking water. According to Leviticus 16:29-31, Moses instituted fasting as an ordinance on the day of atonement, *"This is to be a lasting ordinance for you: On the tenth day of the seventh month you must deny yourselves and not do any work—whether native-born or a foreigner residing among you because on this day atonement will be made for you, to cleanse you. Then, before the Lord, you will be clean from all your sins. It is a day of sabbath rest, and you must deny yourselves; it is a lasting ordinance.*

Moses and Aaron frequently fasted, and Joshua continued the practice when they died. Fasting later became common practice among the Israelites because they viewed it as a way to touch the Heart of God.

Many kings throughout the Bible fasted. King Jehoshaphat is infamous for his extraordinary example of fasting and prayer when a great army came against him. King David fasted for the life of his newborn child with Bathsheba. Even King Ahab fasted when Elijah warned him that judgment was coming upon his household. Jesus fasted in the wilderness for forty day,s and the apostles fasted. The practice of fasting is commonplace among believers, but many people do not understand what it really is.

What is Fasting?

To fast successfully, you must understand what it is and how to do it. Fasting is more than abstaining from food. It is a call to be set apart or sanctified for the master's use. We can describe fasting in various ways, but simply put, it is really a bending of the human will to conform to the will of God. It means to humble ourselves in repentance and obedience to the will of God.

Fasting is not a command, but an ordinance, given by God to cleanse and humble the soul. There is more than one definition for the word ordinance, but one that applies here is; a prescribed usage, practice, or ceremony. Leviticus 16:29-31 details the ordinance of the fasting practice for us. We should humble ourselves and not work while the priest makes atonement for us. Jesus, our great high priest, has already made atonement for us, so when we fast, we only apply the prescribed method of humility to connect with the sacrifice that was already made for us.

Fasting is a tool of deliverance, a pathway for healing, an instrument of repentance, the ultimate act of humility, and an act of worship. Fasting unlocks the power of God in our lives and helps us to interact with The Holy Spirit on a deeper level. When used as a tool of deliverance, fasting enables you to access the power and authority of God to fight on your behalf during times of oppression or danger. We are going to explore many examples throughout the Bible when God delivers his people because they fast and prayed.

The secret to the atomic power of fasting is the bending of the human will to divinely align with the will of God. When our will is in divine alignment with God, His power flows in and through our lives unhindered.

Fasting is acknowledging that we have sinned and humbling ourselves before God, expressing deep sorrow or anguish over our sins, confessing and repenting, and asking for His forgiveness. Asking for help from someone you have wronged requires a lot of humility. No mere mortal can sufficiently cleanse themselves to meet God's requirement for holiness, so we must ask Him to cleanse us, although He is the one we sinned against. When your soul is expressing deep sorrow or anguish, you will have no desire for food, resulting in a natural state of fasting.

Fasting is like a spiritual detox. It does not just detoxify your natural body; it cleanses the soul. We must allow God to expose the hidden things in our hearts, including rejection, jealousy, selfishness, fear, malice, and pride, and allow him to cleanse our hearts.

Fasting is an act of worship, honor, and reverence for God. The Merriam-Webster dictionary describes worship as an act of extravagant respect, honor, admiration, or devotion to someone of high esteem. Therefore, fasting is an extreme act of worship that demonstrates your ardent love and reverence for God. Your worship through fasting touches the heart of God and makes your fasting acceptable to Him. The truest form of fasting that touches the heart of God is when we put God's will above our own. The greatest expression of love for God is to completely lay down your desires for His desires.

Fasting is extreme self-control; it is restraining ourselves from fulfilling the desires of the flesh to obtain the desires of the Spirit. Everyone can fast in some kind of way because there are many ways to deny our fleshly desires. You can fast from food, entertainment, sexual or other natural pleasures. It matters not so much about what you fast as to why you fast.

Reasons to Fast

We should fast because God instituted it as a permanent ordinance. Some say that it is an Old Testament ordinance and does not apply to us today. Jesus fasted, and He instructs us in Matthew 6:17 to wash our faces and anoint our heads *when we fast*. This implies that Jesus expects us to follow the same principles of self-denial and fasting.

Another reason to fast is the desire to please the Lord. Jesus puts it this way: *"Do wedding guests fast while celebrating with the groom? Of course not. They can't fast while the groom is with them. But someday the groom will be taken away from them, and then they will fast."* (Mark 2:19-20). The bridegroom is no longer with us, therefore we should fast because we love him and want to be with Him. These kinds of fasting are Holy Spirit led because of our deep desire to know the Lord.

Another reason to fast is to ask for protection, especially when facing danger. There are many examples of people in the Bible who fasted and prayed for protection. When Ezra returned to Jerusalem, he fasted and asked God for safe passage, and God answered his prayer. Esther the Jewish people fasted for protection when Haman issued a death decree against them and God protected them.

We can also fast for a desired blessing, as Hannah did when she fasted and prayed to conceive a child. While food and intimacy rank as two of the most potent human desires, sometimes greater desires of the heart can override those desires of the flesh, thrusting us into an automatic fast, as with Hannah. Her desire for a child was greater than food or intimacy, therefore, she fasted and prayed and God gave her a child.

Some people fast simply to receive revelation from the Lord. Fasting was the secret of Daniel's many revelations in the Bible. He did not fast because he was in distress, but because he wanted to receive revelation from God. Fasting gives you the confidence and revelation of how to exercise your God-given authority over the situation.

Fasting is sometimes a required addition to prayer, as Jesus told his disciples in Matthew 17:22. *Some things do not go out except through fasting and prayer.* Fasting can significantly enhance prayer because it cleanses the soul and helps you become more aware of God's presence.

Prayer is more than simply asking for something; it is communicating with God and listening to Him respond to you. Prayer is the foundation of our relationship with God, so we should be in tune with our spiritual senses when we pray.

Fasting increases your spiritual awareness and your focus during prayer. So if you are having difficulties accessing the presence of God in prayer, add some fasting to your prayer.

Kinds of Fasting

There are three main types of food fasting: complete, partial, and intermittent. Complete fasting is the absence of food. Partial fasting excludes certain food groups, and intermittent fasting does not restrict what you eat, only when you eat it. Intermittent and partial fasting are great options for people who cannot go without food for extended periods. People who cannot do a complete food fast can fast intermittently or partially. They can also fast from other things such as entertainment, social media, TV, sex, or certain beverages.

People fast for various reasons or for varying amounts of time, such as one day, three days, a week, ten days, twenty-one days, and forty days. You can fast alone or in a group setting with friends or colleagues. It is easier to fast with a friend if your church is not doing a corporate fast, but sometimes you must fast alone.

You can mix up the fast, especially for those of you who desire to fast for longer periods. You can start with an intermittent or partial fast and end with a complete fast. For example, some people did ten days of juice fast, ten days of intermittent, ten days of partial, and ten days of water fasting for their forty-day fasting. Based on your purpose for fasting and guidance from the Holy Spirit, choose which kind of fast works best for you over the next 21 days. I also recommend talking to your doctor before attempting longer periods of fasting.

Acceptable Fast

The key to fasting successfully is to seek the Heart of God and to understand what He calls an acceptable fast. The acceptable fast described in Isaiah 58 shows us how to distinguish between the right and wrong ways to fast and how to correct them. Therefore, we will discuss the right and wrong ways to fast so we can learn what to do and what not to do. We will also discuss why some biblical people fasted and prayed and got results while others did not.

Nowadays, people fast for reasons such as losing weight, detoxifying the body, or obtaining favor from the Lord, but rarely do they fast just to connect with the Heart of God. We have made fasting a self-seeking tool instead of a tool of self-denial. That is the root of the problem and the reason we do not get the results we desire when we fast. The motive behind your fast will have a tremendous impact on your results.

Some people fast to seek justice, some fast for revenge, some fast get obtain favors from the Lord, while others fast simply because they love God. Even though you won't always know the motives of your heart as you fast, if your desire is to please God, He will help you correct your motives.

Public vs. Private Fast

Another thing that makes our fast acceptable is doing it privately. There is a time for public fasting and a time for private fasting. God does not want us to walk around with our heads hanging down and a sad countenance so that people can see that we are fasting. We do not need to advertise that we are fasting; the matter is between us and God. Jesus said, *"But you, when you fast, anoint your head and wash your face, so that you do not appear to men to be fasting, but to your father who is in the secret place; and your Father who sees in secret will reward you openly"* (Matthew 6:17-18). A true fast is not about wearing sackcloth and ashes, nor does it mean bowing our heads to appear that we are fasting, it is to turn our hearts to seek the Heart of God.

Public fasting is acceptable to God when done for the right reason and with inward convictions. God told the nation of Israel to fast as a public act of repentance on the day of atonement. When national disaster looms, the people would gather before the Lord's temple and publicly fast. This type of fasting should take place collectively and publicly before God. However, the Israelites later performed public acts of fasting for others to see that they were fasting. They were going through the motions with no inward convictions.

We are all guilty of this because we go through the routine of fasting each year, but with no inner convictions. The fast we observe has become nothing more than a physical ritual with no inward convictions. Fasting is not an external act, but an inward attitude of the heart. It is the state and posture of our heart that determines whether our fasting is acceptable to God. Acceptable fast includes genuine repentance for breaking God's laws. Sincere repentance occurs when we recognize our fallen state, God's sovereignty, and His goodness. Repentance is a change of heart; it's a decision to humble ourselves and choose God's will over our will.

Humility makes your fast acceptable to God. In Psalms 35:13, King David said he *"put on sackcloth and humbled himself by fasting."* Humbled himself means that he recognized and surrendered to God's divine plan for his life. Humility is acknowledging and embracing our complete dependence on God.

In contrast to humility, pride causes us to disobey God's commandments. Pride is a refusal to accept and follow God's instructions. I Peter 5:5 says, *"God opposes the proud but gives grace to the humble."* When we turn away from his instructions, it causes God to oppose our actions. We must recognize we are at the mercy of God and are not entitled to his blessings. His kindness and mercy make them available to us when we humble ourselves.

Start Your Fasting

Another frequently asked question is, how do I begin and end my fast? People should start fasting mentally before starting the actual fast. Decide what kind of fasting you will do, how long you will do it, and how you will deal with the headaches that, fatigue, and withdrawal symptoms that are usually associated with fasting.

Some people say that they rest, read the word, pray or worship during these symptoms. Everyone's body is different. Do what's best for you, but don't focus on the symptoms; focus on the Lord. These symptoms will gradually fade as the fasting progresses. To ease your body into fasting mode, you can drink non-acidic juice, sports drinks, broth, or water during the fast.

Plan your fasting, and get rid of food items that are a temptation for you prior to starting the fast. Plan to limit your time away from home if possible. Do an intermittent fast a few days before you begin an extended fasting, such as a 21 or 40-day fast, eat smaller portions, and restrict your eating time. Then remove one meal per day until you start the fast.

Also, prepare to face spiritual opposition from the adversary. He will try to tempt you in every way to quit fasting. If you fail, don't stay down. Get back up and try again. Fast a day or two longer to make up for the day or days that you failed. Remember, Jesus fell on his way to Calvary, but He got back up and completed the journey.

The devil will also use situations or people close to you in order to stir up strife and discontentment to distract you. He may even tell you that the fast is not working, but remember; he is the father of lies. So, be on your guard and pray about everything. If your children act out of character, unexpected expenses, or family problems arise, pray about it while keeping your focus on the purpose of your fasting.

Keeping a mental picture of why you are fasting is also essential. This will help you, especially on those tough days when you feel like giving up. Journal your reasons or motives because writing things down helps you to keep them in your focus. What do you want from God? What does God want from you? Is your fasting acceptable to God? If you keep these three things in focus, you will make it to the finish line.

Ending Your Fasting

Breaking your fast requires the same level of self-discipline that you used when you first began it. You will be tempted to eat everything in sight once your appetite awakens, which could cause discomfort and digestive issues. It is best not to eat a heavy meal the moment you break your fast. During the fast, your stomach has been hibernating, so begin with light foods and gradually return to your regular meals. Consider starting with tea, soup, salad, a sandwich, or a smoothie. It is like giving your stomach a little wake-up call to ease its way out of hibernation.

After you complete the fast, refrain from strenuous activities for a few days. You are more susceptible to muscle strains after a prolonged fast because of the lack of protein during the fast. Sometimes, your body may take a few days to regain its full strength, depending on your health conditions prior to the fast.

The enemy will always try to tempt you, just as he did not to Jesus in the wilderness. Therefore, you must conclude your fast with prayer and communion. Remain alert spiritually, especially for the first seven days after your fast. If you fast successfully, you will emerge from your fast in the power of the Holy Spirit.

Benefits of Fasting

Fasting has many natural and spiritual healing benefits; it relieves the body of toxic food buildup, which leads to natural healing. Fasting reduces blood sugar levels, high blood pressure, and weight loss and improves sleep. If you are on medications, be mindful of the effects of fasting. I do not intend this information or any other aspect of this book as medical advice. Before starting a fast, you should always discuss any medical concerns with your doctor. Although we will discuss some health benefits of fasting, this book emphasizes the spiritual benefits of fasting because we often overlook them in pursuit of the physical benefits of fasting.

What to Expect

As you fast, expect to encounter God in dreams, visions, prophecies, and revelations from God as you journey through the Heart of God. I suggest reading a chapter a day and reflecting on its revelations as you fast and pray.

Your goal should not be to lose weight or to solve problems during this fast but to experience intimacy with God. This fast is a sacred pathway to connect with the Heart of God, and if you treat it any less, you will shortchange yourself.

I will first explore fasting through the lens of Joel 2 and Isaiah 58 fast. Then I will analyze the prophetic connection between fasting and prayer through each biblical fast while focusing on how they fasted and prayed. And lastly, I will also review the various benefits and rewards of fasting.

As we explore each biblical fast, we will pause to observe how each person or nation successfully touched the heart of God through prophetic fasting. I hope you will glean fasting insights that will help you successfully touch the Heart of God.

I

Biblical Fasting

This section of the book analyzes 28 biblical fasting that touches the heart of God that was prompted by the prophetic messages or released the prophetic messages.

1

Blow the Trumpet

Blow the trumpet in Zion, consecrate a fast, call a sacred assembly; gather the people, sanctify the congregation, assemble the elders, gather the children and nursing babes; let the bridegroom go out from his chamber and the bride from her dressing room. Let the priests, who minister to the Lord, Weep between the porch and the altar; Let them pray, "Spare Your people, O Lord, And do not give Your heritage to reproach, That the nations should rule over them. Why should they say among the peoples, 'Where is their God?'" (Joel 2:15-17).

I dreamed that two warplanes were surveying an enormous gaping hole in the middle of a city. One pilot said to the other, "Let's go to the Middle East. We will come back the day after tomorrow." The gaping hole in the ground appears to be ground zero in New York City. It was about twilight, and some high-rise buildings in the city were lit. It felt like something sinister was about to happen because no cars or people were on the streets.

A man crossed the street discreetly by bending low and hiding behind anything he could. He walked up the steps to the front door of a house and knocked in a coded manner. Another man partially opened the door and conversed with him in an urgent, whispered conversation. The man who crossed the street said, "We need to take action before the warplanes return the day after tomorrow." The other man replied, "We still have tomorrow to discuss this," said the man who crossed the street. "Tomorrow is not promised to anyone, so we should start planning now." The two men continued the discussion as they crossed the street and entered a high-rise building.

Is there a possibility that another terrorist attack like September 11 is being planned for America? I do not know, but one thing I know for sure, it's time to blow the trumpet in America and call a solemn assembly. This dream puzzled me greatly until I read Johnathan Cahn's book, *The Harbinger.* I understood the Lord is really blowing a trumpet across America, calling us back to repentance because judgment is decreed against America. So as we break open the Joel chapter two fast, let's observe and apply the recommendations of the prophet. We will explore each exhortation as it relates to fasting and its prophetic significance.

Blow the Trumpet

Joel, chapter two, presents several prophetic exhortations with an urgent call to fasting. First, Joel exhorted the people to *"blow the trumpet in Zion, proclaim a fast, and call a sacred assembly."* In Bible days, the sound of the trumpet was a divine disruption of everyday life because the people had to stop whatever they were doing and gather at the temple.

In times of disaster, we recognize our human limitations and God's sovereignty. Many people saw the pandemic as God's trumpet, warning us to repent because it completely disrupted our lives and exposed our limitations and complete dependence on God. Despite the physical closures of churches, some people gathered virtually and prayed fervently, while others mocked. In every move of God, there will always be mixed reactions. Our response to God's trumpets determines whether we encounter His judgment or mercy. We can avoid many painful situations in our lives if we learn to recognize God's trumpets. When we hear or recognize God's trumpets in our lives, it is important for us to respond and react accordingly. The sound of the trumpet is God's grace and mercy, calling us to consecrate a fast and call a sacred assembly.

Consecrate a Fast

Secondly, the prophet told the priest to consecrate a fast and call a solemn assembly. The priest usually declared fasting only on the day of atonement, but judgment was coming, and the people needed to atone for their sins through fasting and prayer. Usually, this kind of fast is an absolute fast, with no food or drink, and typically ranges from twenty-four hours to three days, as was the case when the people of Nineveh fasted to avert judgment. To consecrate a fast means people had to cease their daily routine, assemble before Go,d and pray.

A sacred assembly usually takes place on two occasions, on the designated feast days or days of pending disaster. In this case, disaster was pending, and both young and old, rich and poor, needed to assemble before the Lord. Joel exhorts the priest to *"Gather the people, sanctify the congregation, assemble the elders, gather the children and nursing babes; Let the bridegroom go out from his chamber, and the bride from her dressing room."* (Joel 2:16). According to Deuteronomy 16:8, a sacred assembly is one in which the people would assemble before the Lord, refrain from work, read the laws of God and recommit themselves to obeying them. This gathering was not one of joy and laughter, but one of sorrow and sadness as people realized their sins and repented.

People's response to God's warning today is alarming, given what happened to Israel when they refused to repent. God wanted to forgive

Israel's sins and spare them from judgment, but they refused to heed God's warning, and their nation went into exile. God is holding out his hands to us today as He did for Israel because He delights in showing mercy. We must turn away from our sinful practices and assemble ourselves in fasting and prayer to obtain His mercy and forgiveness.

Weep and Pray

Next, the prophet Joel instructed the priests to weep between the porch and the altar. *Let the priests, who minister to the Lord, Weep between the porch and the altar; Let them pray, "Spare Your people, O Lord, and do not give Your heritage to reproach, that the nations should rule over them. Why should they say among the peoples, Where is their God?"* (Joel 2:17). The priests were to dress in mourning clothes and spend the night at the altar weeping, repenting because they had no grain or wine to offer to God (see Joel 1:13).

God cut off their grain supply because they were using them to worship idols. When confronted with this evil, the people stated, *"We will do whatever we want." We will burn incense and pour out liquid offerings to the Queen of Heaven just as much as we like—just as we, and our ancestors, and our kings and officials have always done in the towns of Judah and in the streets of Jerusalem. For in those days, we had plenty to eat, and we were well off and had no troubles!"* (Jeremiah 44:17).

Despite many prophetic warnings, the people refused to listen to the prophets; therefore, God pronounced judgment. The Lord revealed the terrible day of judgment to the prophet Joel and told him to warn the people because He wanted them to repent. Joel urged the people to return to God with all their hearts, fasting, weeping, and mourning. (see Joel 2:12-13). They were to weep because they were breaking the heart of God, who loves them unconditionally.

Rend your Heart

One of the unexpected things we will encounter as we journey through the heart of God is the broken part. It never occurred to me that God could have a broken heart. I mean, He is God. How could His heart be broken? Then He said to me a heart that has never been broken does not know how to love. God created us to live in a divine intimate relationship with His people, but when we break His laws, we break His heart. His laws are guidelines that facilitate this heart-to-heart relationship with us. That's why God told the people, *"Return to Me with all your heart."* The heart refers to the center or the innermost part of our being. A heart-to-heart relationship with God is like a marital relationship; we promise our fidelity to Him in worship. We breach His trust when we stray away from our first love. We can only regain His trust by returning to God with sincere sorrow and asking His forgiveness.

In Bible days, it was customary for people to tear their clothes while fasting, but some people did so with no inward convictions. They were tearing their clothes, but their hearts were not grieving over the things that broke God's heart. Therefore, the prophet told the people, *"Rend your heart and not your garments. Return to the LORD your God, for he is compassionate, slow to anger, and abounding in love, and he relents from sending calamity.* (Joel 2:13). God is not interested in meaningless sacrifices or acts of service. *The sacrifices God desires are a broken spirit and a contrite heart* (Psalm 51:17). He is interested in a pure heart that is faithful to Him.

When someone breaks our hearts, they can buy us gifts and do lots of nice things for us, but if they never express sorrow and a desire for reconciliation, we rarely get back into a relationship with them. When God says to rend our hearts, He wants us to acknowledge our sins, express our sorrow for breaking his heart, and seek reconciliation because He is merciful and will graciously forgive those who confess and repent.

Everyone wants to believe their hearts are pure; however, we are unaware of many things buried deep within. Pride often prevents us from acknowledging our sins and returning to God. Pride tells us we have done nothing wrong and therefore do not need to repent. According to Jeremiah 17:9-10, *"The heart is deceitful above all things, and desperately wicked; Who can know it? I, the LORD, search the heart, I test the mind, even to give every man according to his ways, according to the fruit of his doings."*

Satan uses the pain and suffering that we go through to sow seeds of bitterness, fear, rejection, pride, maliciousness, envy, jealousy, lust, discontentment, dissension, violence, etc. Only God can search the hidden depths of our hearts and help us uproot those evil tares. Our only hope for a pure heart is to give God all our hearts. He already knows our hearts are deceitful, but if we give Him our hearts, He will purify them and make them good. Apart from God, nothing good lives in our sinful hearts.

Nothing Good in Me

Several years ago, I had an argument with someone and said some things that I should not have said. I tried to pray as usual, but I couldn't. The only words that came to my mind were, "God, you cannot use me for ministry; use someone else; just let me be a doormat in your kingdom." I suddenly saw a vision of myself sitting on a park bench, and Jesus was sitting across from me on another park bench. With tears in my eyes, I looked right into His liquid, brown, glinting, heavenly eyes and said, "Lord, nothing good lives in me." He replied, "I know, but I am in you, and I am good enough for both of us." At that moment, freedom and joy filled my heart. Despite my mistakes, Jesus still lives within me, so I immediately forgave those who hurt me.

Years after this experience, I came across Romans 8:17: *"I know that nothing good lives in me, that is in my sinful nature. I want to do what is right, but I can't."* God doesn't live in our hearts based on our righteousness but based on the cross. Our sinful nature resists giving all our hearts to the Lord because *"The sinful nature is always hostile to God. It never obeyed God's laws, and it never will, but those who are still under the control of their sinful nature can never please God, but your sinful nature does not control you. The Holy Spirit controls you if you have the Spirit of God living in you."* (Romans 8:7-9, emphasis added). We must make a conscious decision to give God all our hearts because the enemy controls any part of our hearts that we do not surrender to God.

Call to Action

As in the days of the prophet Joel, people have turned away from God and are turning to idol worshiping, witchcraft, and all kinds of perversions. Despite these terrible sins, God is still blowing a trumpet, calling people to repentance so that He can save them from impending judgment.

So, as you fast and pray today, let us take a moment to consider the prophetic warning signs in our lives and our nation. Pain, sorrows, lawlessness, wars, and plagues are God's trumpets calling us to repentance. Let us rend our hearts and return to God in fasting, weeping, and mourning. Let us give Him all of our broken, bleeding hearts and allow Him to heal them.

Let us blow a trumpet, proclaim a fast and call a solemn assembly. You can blow the trumpet with your gifts and talents, join a prayer group, offer encouragement, or sing a song. When you sense the Holy Spirit moving in your heart, grab your phone and blow your trumpet, post something encouraging on social media, text or call somebody and ask them to join you in fasting and prayer.

PROMISE. *And also, on My menservants and My maidservants, I will pour out My Spirit in those days* (Joel 2:29).

2

Tell My People Their Sins

"Shout with the voice of a trumpet blast. Shout aloud! Don't be timid. Tell my people Israel of their sins! Yet they act so piously! They come to the Temple every day and seem delighted to learn all about me. They act like a righteous nation that would never abandon the laws of its God. They ask me to take action on their behalf, pretending they want to be near me." (Isaiah 58:1-2).

Have you ever fasted and prayed, but nothing happens? This is exactly how the people of Isaiah's days felt. They were decent churchgoers who did everything they were supposed to do, worshiped, prayed, fasted, and offered sacrifices regularly, but there was something wrong. They were going through the motions of fasting but complained that God was not answering their prayers. *"We have fasted before you!' they say. 'Why aren't you impressed? We have been very hard on ourselves, and you don't even notice it!'* So in Isaiah 58:3-4, God instructed the Prophet to tell the people that their prayers were not being answered because they were fasting to please themselves and were oppressing their workers while they were fasting. He also accused them of fasting for strife and debate and striking with the fist of wickedness. So he told them you

11

cannot fast in this manner if you want your voice to be heard on high.

You may have experienced times when you didn't feel God was listening to your prayers or noticing your fasting. Perhaps you prayed for someone's healing, and they weren't healed, or maybe you prayed for a blessing and didn't receive it. You have even asked God the same question these people are asking: *why are you not impressed with our fasting?* God's answer to those people back in Isaiah's time may still be true for us today. God gave them a list of things that displeased him during their fast.

Pleasure Fasting

God first told them, "When you fast, you find pleasure." The people participated in some sort of pleasurable activity on the day of their fasting, which should be a solemn occasion. Leviticus 16:31 says *Fasting is a Sabbath of solemn rest to you, and you shall afflict yourselves; it is a statute forever.* Indulging in pleasure on the day of our fast does not demonstrate genuine sorrow over our sins or sincere devotion to God. Pleasure can be anything that does not require self-denial. When we fast, we should limit our pleasure activities to the bare necessities on fasting days. The best way to avoid pleasure during your fast would be to prepare before you begin the fast. Adjust your schedule if necessary, discuss it with your spouse, make purchases in advance, and develop a mental attitude of self-denial.

Oppressing your Workers

The next thing that caused their fasting to be unacceptable to God was exploiting their workers. God gave them specific laws against such behaviors. Deuteronomy 24:14-15 says, *"Do not take advantage of a hired worker who is poor and needy, whether that worker is a fellow Israelite or a foreigner living in one of your towns. Pay them their wages each day before sunset because they are poor and are counting on it. Otherwise, they may cry to the Lord against you, and you will be guilty of sin.*" In order for their fast to be accepted, they needed to obey God's commandments and stop oppressing their workers. We cannot truly humble ourselves before God by fasting while breaking His laws. We should always pay people their fair wages, and God will reward us for faithfully adhering to His commandments.

Revenge

Another reason that their fast did not impress the Lord was that they were doing it to seek revenge. They wanted God to strike their enemies. One example of fasting for revenge is found in I Samuel 14:24 "*The men of Israel were distressed that day, for Saul had placed the people under oath, saying, 'Cursed is the man who eats any food until the evening before I have taken vengeance on my enemies.' So, none of the people tasted food.*" King Saul didn't call the fast to seek direction or protection from God. He was not even trying to bow down in reverence or humility to touch the Heart of God; all he wanted was revenge.

It is okay to fast and ask God for relief from our afflictions, but we should not fast for revenge. God is the only one righteous enough to exact vengeance, and He gives everyone time to repent. Romans 12:19 *Do not avenge yourselves, beloved, but leave room for God's wrath. For it is written: "Vengeance is Mine; I will repay, says the Lord."* Do not fast for revenge; pray for your enemies, give your pain to God, and allow Him to heal you. We must follow Jesus' example of forgiveness; His accusers beat and crucified Him, but He prayed, *"Father, forgive them, for they don't know what they are doing."* (Luke 23:34). Let go of any desire for justice, revenge, strife, or debate. God has better plans for you than what you are trying to obtain through revenge. Besides, the purpose of fasting is not revenge; it is to touch God's heart. After God told them what was preventing him from answering their prayers, he told them how to correct their actions.

God's Chosen Fast

God wanted His people to compare the standards of their fasting to His commandments, so He asked them, *"Is this not the fast that I have chosen: To loose the bonds of wickedness, to undo the heavy burdens, to let the oppressed go free, and that you break every yoke? Is it not to share your bread with the hungry, and that you bring to your house the poor who are cast out? When you see the naked, that you cover him, and not hide from your own flesh?* (Isaiah 58:6-7). God gave them specific laws regarding these practices when they left Egypt. Since the prophet had to remind them of these commandments, they were not being observed. They were not following the laws that God gave them concerning such practices.

Set the Oppress Free

When God told them to loose the bonds of wickedness and set the oppressed free he was referring to false imprisonment and the forgiveness of debt, respectively. Their law at the time was, *"You must not convict anyone of a crime on the testimony of only one witness. They must establish the facts of the case by the testimony of two or three witnesses."* (**Deuteronomy 19:15**). Obviously, they were falsely imprisoning people and as such was not practicing the laws that God gave them.

The forgiveness of debt was an ordinance for the Israelites from the days of Moses. Deuteronomy 15:1-2 says, *"At the end of every seven years, you must cancel debts. This is how it is to be done: every creditor shall cancel any loan they have made to a fellow Israelite. They shall not require payment from anyone among their own people because the Lord's time for canceling debts has been proclaimed."* They should cancel debts every seven years, but they stopped practicing this ordinance and were exacting payment from their fellow Israelites.

Break the Yoke

These yokes were literally chains of slavery. God's laws say that they should release their slaves at the end of every six years. Deuteronomy 15:12 says, *"If any of your people—Hebrew men or women—sell themselves to you and serve you six years, in the seventh year, you must let them go free."* They were not keeping that commandment because the prophet Jeremiah also warned them of this great wickedness. *"This is what the Lord, the God of Israel, says: I made a covenant with your ancestors when I brought them out of Egypt, out of the land of slavery. I said, 'Every seventh year, each of you must free any fellow Hebrews who have sold themselves to you. After they have served you six years, you must let them go free.' Your ancestors, however, did not listen to me or pay attention to me."* (Jeremiah 34:13-14). This thing was very detestable to God and caused the whole nation to end up in captivity.

We may not be enslaving anyone, but manipulation and control are forms of mental slavery, and it's not pleasing to God. That was the same spirit behind Jezebel's actions in Israel; another name for it is witchcraft. Never seek to control or manipulate other people's lives; seek instead to inspire and motivate them. Allow people to be who God intends them to be, not who you want them to be, including your spouse and children.

Help the Needy

Helping the needy was also an ordinance that God gave them when they came out of Egypt. Deuteronomy 15:7- 8 says, *"If anyone is poor among your fellow Israelite in any of the towns of the land the Lord your God is giving you, do not be hardhearted or tightfisted toward them. Instead, be openhanded and freely lend them whatever they need.* This was a command that God gave them; it was not optional. He told them, in Deuteronomy 15:11, *"There will always be poor people in the land. Therefore, I command you to be openhanded toward your fellow Israelites who are poor and needy in your land.* He even told them that if they refuse to help the needy and the needy cry out to Him, they will be guilty of sin. So their sins

15

were preventing them from getting answers to their prayers, although they were fasting.

In Isaiah 58:7, God instructed the people to feed the hungry and shelter the homeless, *give clothes to those who need them, and do not hide from relatives who need your help.*" The people likely walked to the temple daily to fast and pray, passing the poor on the street but turning their backs on them. We should always strive to show kindness to those in need because it is the best way to express the love of God. James 1:27 says, *"Religion that God our Father accepts as pure and faultless is this: to look after orphans and widows in their distress and to keep oneself from being polluted by the world."* And remember Matthew 6:2-4 says, *"When you give to the needy, do not announce it with trumpets, as the hypocrites do in the synagogues and on the streets, to be honored by others. Truly, I tell you, they have received their reward in full. But when you give to the needy, do not let your left hand know what your right hand is doing so that your giving may be in secret. Then your Father, who sees what is done in secret, will reward you.* When we give to those in need, it touches the heart of God.

Keep the Sabbath Holy

The last thing God told the people that would make their fasting acceptable to Him was, *"Keep the Sabbath day holy. Don't pursue your own interests on that day, but enjoy the Sabbath and speak of it with delight as the Lord's holy day. Honor the Sabbath in everything you do on that day and don't follow your own desires or talk idly."* (Isaiah 58:13). The sabbath day is very important to God because it is a holy day of rest and reflection. A day to stop all our work and focus on the Lord. So how do you keep the Sabbath? Exodus 20:9-11 gives us the guidelines for the Sabbath, *"Six days you shall labor and do all your work, but the seventh day is a sabbath to the Lord your God. On it, you shall not do any work, neither you, your son or daughter, your male or female servant, your animals, or any foreigner residing in your towns. For in six days, the Lord made the heavens and the earth, the sea, and all that is in them, but he rested on the seventh day. Therefore, the Lord blessed the Sabbath day and made it holy."*

Unfortunately, in our society, the Sabbath has become a forgotten religious relic of the past. God still requires people to keep the Sabbath, not for salvation, but to enjoy intimate fellowship with Him. You can choose which day to rest; Sabbath does not necessarily mean Saturday because the Bible says six days you shall labor, but it didn't tell us which six days. If you have a job that requires you to work on Saturdays, choose a day in the week as your day of rest and reflection. God is not so concerned with the day as with your heart. He wants us to set aside a day of rest because it tells God that we love and honor him. The Sabbath is like a 'date night' between God and man. It is time set aside to rekindle our intimacy with God. One of the greatest joys of God's heart is for us to find joy in spending time with Him.

When our hearts are more concerned with accomplishment than intimacy with God, we do not rest. Failing to keep the Sabbath is a great dishonor to God for two reasons: We do not trust Him to supply all our needs, and we do not esteem Him highly enough to desire intimacy with him. It is like having a spouse but sharing no intimacy with him or her. You do everything together, but there is no intimacy in the relationship. What kind of marriage would that be?

When you rest from your work, you are telling God; I trust you; I know I can't work for all I need, but I know you will supply them even when I rest. Remember, Jesus said, *"The Sabbath was made for man, not man for the Sabbath. So the Son of Man is Lord even of the Sabbath."* (Mark 2:27-28). When Jesus said He is Lord of the Sabbath, it means He created the Sabbath for his purpose. He does not serve the Sabbath; the Sabbath serves Him. Since the Sabbath was made for man and not man for the Sabbath, it serves us and not the other way around.

We are to make it a priority to rest from our labor so that we can be restored and refreshed in the presence of the Lord.

Call to Action

We fast and pray today, hoping that God will notice, but like the Israelites, we are breaking God's rules. We seek Him for answers to our problems and are confused when He does not respond. Sometimes, the issues we face result from our disobedience. Many people choose to disobey God's commandments yet claim that they love Him. Jesus said, *"If you love Me, keep My commandments."* (John 14:15). Only through keeping His commandments can we express genuine love for God.

The church has become more about socializing than seeking God. Pastoral messages are now nothing more than a motivational fix for the week. Worship service becomes entertainment, prayer becomes a chore, and fasting is only for weight loss or to ask God for a breakthrough. We are no longer aware of our sins because our carnal desires impede the tenderness of our conscience. Only when God withholds His blessings do we realize that our motives for seeking God are impure.

So as you fast today, be mindful of any prophetic instruction you have received personally or for your family or nation, and pray them back to God. Repent from breaking his commandments, and do not fast to seek revenge or for strife and debate. Let God become your pleasure, your greatest delight. Keep the Sabbath and do any corresponding actions God tells you to do. Help the needy, pray for those who hurt and abuse you, forgive them, and God will reward you openly.

PROMISE: *Then your light shall break forth like the morning, your healing shall spring forth speedily, and your righteousness shall go before you; The glory of the Lord shall be your rear guard.* (Isaiah 58:8).

3

Moses Fast

And I fell down before the Lord, as at the first, forty days and forty nights; I neither ate bread nor drank water, because of all your sin which you committed in doing wickedly in the sight of the Lord, to provoke Him to anger. For I was afraid of the anger and hot displeasure with which the Lord was angry with you, to destroy you. But the Lord listened to me at that time also." (Deuteronomy 9: 18-19)

This is one of the most incredible Fasts recorded in the Bible. Moses fasted for a total of eighty days in two increments of forty days each. While Moses was on the mountain with the Lord for the first forty-day fast, the Lord told him to go back down the mountain because the people sinned by worshiping the golden calf, and I am angry enough to destroy them all.

Moses descended from the mountain and destroyed the golden calf. Then he returned to the mountain for another forty days of fasting and repentance. Each fasting was conducted for two different purposes and resulted in different outcomes; however, both fast resulted in prophetic instructions from the Lord.

First Forty-day Fast

In the first fasting, *"Moses entered the cloud as he went up the mountain and stayed on the mountain for forty days and forty nights. (Exodus 24:18)*. During this time of consecration, Moses received the prophetic instructions and revelations to build the Tabernacle; he received the ten commandments and the laws to govern the people. During this time, Moses saw the pattern of the Tabernacle and received divine guidance to lead the people.

This must have been one of the most glorious experiences Moses ever had. Nothing can compare with being in such a glorious presence of The Lord. It's the thing that most of us desire when we say that we are seeking the heart of God. We want to know what the Lord desires of us. We want to see Him in his glory and for Him to reveal glorious things to us.

While Moses was having this glorious experience on the mountain of God, the people grew impatient, waiting for his return. The people grew tired of waiting for Moses to come down from the mountain with instructions from the Lord. They thought God had abandoned them. *When the people saw that Moses was so long in coming down from the mountain, they gathered around Aaron and said, "Come, make us gods who will go before us. As for this fellow Moses who brought us up out of Egypt, we don't know what has happened to him."(Exodus 32:1)*. It is hard to believe that these were the same people who saw the ten plagues, the parting of the red sea, the bitter water turned sweet, the manna and quail, the water from a rock, the pillar of cloud by day, the pillar of fire by night, and the fire on the mountain. How could they turn away from God so quickly? What could a golden calf do for them that God could not do? After all that God did for them, they turned and gave their worship to an idol. Imagine how revolting that must have been to the glorious God who gave them life and holds their breath in His hands.

20

They praised God when He delivered them from Egypt, and they feared Him when he appeared to them on Mount Sinai, but in just forty days of their leader's absence, they had turned away from Him. It seems that as long as they could see God's miracles, they worshiped Him, but when God was silent, they reverted to idols.

The Lord told Moses, *"Now, therefore, let Me alone that My wrath may burn hot against them, and I may consume them. And I will make of you a great nation."* Moses refused (Exodus 32:10). Moses pleaded with God to remember the covenant with their forefathers and to forgive the people's sins. Here we see Moses acting as the prophet and the priest. He received the prophetic word of judgment but acted as a priest and interceded for the people.

Many of us do the same thing those people did back then. As long as God keeps providing and protecting us, we will worship, but as soon as we encounter trials, we stop worshiping God and start complaining. We often become impatient, waiting for the things God promised, and we sometimes create golden calves out of our previous blessings. While God's promises may take a long time to come to fruition, we must remain faithful to Him through trials.

Created to Worship God

We are created with the desire to worship, but we often worship the wrong gods. People who do not know God believe they can make their own gods. When we don't recognize who God is, our built-in desire to worship Him will lead us to worship unholy things. That's what Israel did when they built the golden calf; they desired to worship God, but Moses was on the mountain and could not lead them to worship God, so they created an idol. I understand their desire to worship, but where did they get the idea of creating an idol?

While living in Egypt, they learned to worship idols, and some brought their idols with them when God set them free. We see evidence of this many years later as the children of Israel prepared to cross over the river Jordan. Joshua instructed them to get rid of their idols (Joshua 3). It is appalling to think that after forty miraculous years in the wilderness, they stood on the brink of Jordan with idols. And what's more interesting is that although they had idols with them, God still loved them and did wonders among them.

Second Forty-Day Fast

After coming down from the mountain and destroying the golden calf, Moses went back up the mountain to fast and pray for the people's forgiveness. *"The next day, Moses said to the people, "You have committed a great sin. But now I will go up to the Lord; perhaps I can make atonement for your sin." So, Moses went back to the Lord and said, "Oh, what a great sin these people have committed! They have made themselves gods of gold. But now, please forgive their sin—but if not, then blot me out of the book you have written." The Lord replied to Moses, "Whoever has sinned against me, I will blot out of my book. Now go, lead the people to the place I spoke of, and my angel will go before you. However, I will punish them for their sin when the time comes for me to punish."* (Exodus 32:30-34).

Moses consecrated himself and fasted for another forty days to make atonement for the people's sins. Coming out of a forty-day fast and returning to it is difficult, but keep in mind that this was supernatural fasting because Moses was on the mountain of God in the presence of God. The presence of God can preserve us without food. Not only that but Moses served God and His people selflessly and was willing to do whatever it took to protect them.

Moses embraced his job as a shepherd to guide God's lost sheep through the wilderness. His days as a shepherd in the desert prepared him to be a shepherd for the people of Israel. He knew God enough to know that His threats were no idle threats, but he also knew that God's love and mercy are endless. Moses also knew how to touch the heart of God. He confessed the people's sins and pleaded with God for their forgiveness. The Lord granted Moses's request and delayed the punishment for a more suitable time. So, Moses's second fasting yielded another prophetic instruction from the Lord and granted them grace and forgiveness. Leaders like Moses deserve their share of recognition, for the Lord says to give honor to whom honor is due.

Pray for your Leaders

It is very common for us to take the people God sends into our lives for granted. We often neglect God's shepherds and turn to people who sound spiritual but can only offer us a golden calf. Even though Aaron was on the mountain of God and worked alongside Moses to free the people from Egypt, he was not the chosen leader. Aaron also needed to wait for Moses to return from the mountain with instructions from God. It is terrible to be led by a leader who has no direction from God. The Lord did not give Aaron any directives to lead the people, so he should have instructed the people to wait for Moses to return.

It would have been more appropriate for the people to pray for Moses' safe return from the mountain rather than build an idol. It is important to pray for those who provide spiritual guidance because they make tremendous sacrifices to stand in the place of leadership. Moses was even willing to have his name removed from God's book if God did not forgive the people. We should not praise or worship our leaders, but we should honor them. 1 Thessalonians 5:12 says, *"Dear brothers and sisters, honor those who are your leaders in the Lord's work. They work hard among you and give you spiritual guidance."* Although it may take a while to see what God is doing in our leaders' lives, we should pray for them instead of building golden calves and seeking leadership from others who are not anointed to lead.

Call to Action

God loves us even in our sins, regardless of the idols we have in our lives, but He is pleading with us to get rid of those idols and give our hearts entirely to Him.

When you don't know what's next, pray and wait on the Lord. The key to remaining faithful is loving God above all else and recognizing that His plans are still good, even when we don't understand what he is doing.

Another takeaway from Moses' fast is to honor those God uses to speak to you rather than becoming impatient with them. Accept that they can only lead you at the pace God is leading them.

So as you fast and pray today, consider those in leadership over you, pray for them, and be patient with yourself and others. Pray for people in leadership everywhere, from presidents to pastors, because we do not know the tremendous price they pay to be our leaders.

PROMISE: *If you extend your soul to the hungry and satisfy the afflicted soul, then your light shall dawn in the darkness, and your darkness shall be as the noonday.* (Isaiah 58:10).

4

Joshua Fast

"Joshua and the elders of Israel tore their clothing in dismay, threw dust on their heads, and bowed face down to the ground before the Ark of the LORD until evening. Then Joshua cried out, "Ah, Sovereign LORD, why did you bring us across the Jordan River if you are going to let the Amorites kill us? If only we had been content to stay on the other side! Lord, what can I say now that Israel has fled from its enemies? For when the Canaanites and all the other people living in the land hear about it, they will surround us and wipe our name off the face of the earth. And then what will happen to the honor of your great name?" (Joshua 7: 6-9).

Have you ever lost a battle you knew you should have won? When you entered the battle, you were confident of victory, but somehow you lost. It makes no earthly sense to have failed; you trust confidently in God; you prayed and did all the right things, but you did not get the victory. That's exactly where Joshua and the Israelites found themselves. After defeating the great city of Jericho, their next target of conquest was a small city called Ai. Since they were confident of winning, they sent only three thousand men to battle instead of the entire army, but they lost.

When Joshua heard that the armies of Israel fled before their enemies, he tore his clothes and laid prostrate before God from morning until evening. He refused to eat or drink because this was not the outcome he expected from battle. They had already assessed the situation. They knew Ai was a city they could easily capture, but that did not happen.

Joshua and the elders of Israel fasted, and he prayed from morning until evening. *Oh sovereign God, why did you bring us across the Jordan River if you are going to let the Amorites kill us? If only we had been content to stay on the other side. Lord, what can I say now that Israel has fled before its enemies?* (Joshua 7:7). Joshua had done everything right but lost the battle. Joshua knew how to get a hold of God because he had seen Moses do it many times in the wilderness. He laid prostrate before God and refused to eat from morning till evening. He knew the task ahead of them was massive, and they could not do it without the help of God, so he desperately needed to hear from God.

Massive Task

Israel had survived the wilderness and crossed over the river Jordan, conquered the great city of Jericho but suffered defeat by the small city of Ai. They were now in the land of giants and had the massive task of conquering and purging the land. Their commander Joshua knew that failure was not an option; any sign of failure indicated that God was not with them. Joshua knew the people had no confidence to fight against giants; they completely depended on God to help them drive out the nations before them. So, if they fail, something must be wrong because the sovereign God cannot fail.

In contrast to the nations they faced, the Israeli army was very primitive; their only military power was God. They didn't have horses and chariots, and they were few in numbers compared to their enemies.

They were beginning their military campaign to purge the land, so if the surrounding nations heard that the small city of Ai defeated them, other nations could form allies and attack them. The fear of Israel's God was the only thing preventing the surrounding giant nations from attacking them. *When all the Amorite kings west of the Jordan and all the Canaanite kings along the coast heard how the Lord had dried up the Jordan before the Israelites until they had crossed over, their hearts melted in fear, and they no longer had the courage to face the Israelites* (Joshua 5:1). So, the people of Jericho securely shut their gates, no one could enter, and no one could leave because the people were afraid of the Israelites (Joshua 6:1). The people of Jericho were not afraid of the small little nomadic army; they were afraid of Israel's God. Although the Israelites were small in numbers and the odds were against them, they miraculously won the battle of Jericho because their God fought for them. So Joshua understood that the battle belonged to God, and if Israel failed, then God failed, and God cannot fail. Naturally, Joshua fasted and questioned the Lord about this Ai situation.

Question the Lord

Joshua first acknowledged God as sovereign in his prayer because he knew God rules over everything. Sovereign means that there is no one greater than God. Acknowledging the sovereignty of God also means that Joshua recognizes Israel's dependence on God to fight their battles. Joshua had confidence in the sovereign God that he would win every battle every time, so this unexpected defeat confounded him.

Although Joshua was confident in the power of God, he experienced momentary doubt because he did not expect defeat. He wondered if staying on the other side of Jordan was better. He wondered if God would allow the Amorites to destroy them.

Joshua led the military campaign that supernaturally conquered the great city of Jericho; he saw the mighty miracles in the wilderness; he was up on the mountain with Moses in the presence of God. He knew God promised to drive out the inhabitants of the land, but losing the battle caused him to doubt that God was in their midst. God's goodness and sovereignty were not questioned; Joshua did not doubt that God was powerful enough to defeat their enemies. Israel lost a battle that they should have easily won. Joshua wanted to know why the Lord didn't fight for them as He always had. He doubted God was with them because they could not lose the battle if God fought for them.

When Joshua experienced doubt, he turned to God in fasting and prayer, demonstrating his dependence on the Lord for victory. Joshua could have gathered a larger army and gone back and fought Ai rather than fast and pray, but he knew his God and Israel's purpose for crossing Jordan. Joshua knew God did not bring them across the Jordan to destroy them at the hand of the Amorites. Joshua knew that his military strength didn't come from the number of soldiers but from God. He was not trusting in the three thousand men that went into battle but in the God that empowered them. Joshua needed answers because the stakes were too high to accept defeat, so he fasted.

The Answer

After Joshua fasted and prayed, The Lord said to Joshua, *"Stand up! What are you doing down on your face? Israel has sinned; they have violated my covenant, which I commanded them to keep. They have stolen some of the devoted things and put them with their own possessions. That is why the Israelites cannot stand against their enemies; they turn their backs and run because they have been made liable to destruction. I will not be with you anymore unless you destroy whatever among you is devoted to destruction."* Joshua 7: 10-12.

The Lord revealed to Joshua that sin was in the camp and gave him a strategy to reveal who sinned and how to purge the camp. The Lord instructed Joshua to summon the tribes of Israel, and Achan from the tribe of Judah was chosen. Achan sinned by taking a beautiful

Babylonian robe, two hundred shekels of silver, and a bar of gold weighing fifty shekels from Jericho's conquest devoted to destruction.

God previously told them that *the city and all in it are to be devoted to the Lord. Only Rahab, the prostitute, and all who are with her in her house shall be spared because she hid the spies we sent. But keep away from the devoted things so that you will not bring about your own destruction by taking any of them. Otherwise, you will make the camp of Israel liable to destruction and bring trouble on it. All the silver and gold and the articles of bronze and iron are sacred to the Lord and must go into his treasury."* (Joshua 6:17-19).

The people of Israel stoned Achan and his family to death, and God restored His favor to Israel. Although this was a terrible tragedy for Achan and his family, it was a prime example of how one man's sin caused the entire nation to suffer defeat, but one man's death brought salvation to the entire nation.

Achan's death was a prophetic foreshadowing of Jesus; although He didn't sin, he had to die for the nation. In John 11:50, the high priest told the Sanhedrin, *"You do not realize that it is better for you that one man dies for the people than that the whole nation perish."* Like Achan, Adam's sin brought destruction upon humanity, but Jesus' death on the cross brought salvation to the entire world.

What is in your Camp?

Even the most faithful person can experience doubt, especially when they lose a battle they were confident they would win. You will go through circumstances that cause you to feel like God is not with you, especially when you experience defeat by things you should have overcome.

You can always tell when the Spirit of the Lord is not with you; you feel a sense of hopelessness and despair. Sometimes you will feel confused, angry, doubtful, rejected, and forgotten. You feel like God is far from you and pray, but the words seem to fall back on your head. That's an excellent time to add fasting to your prayer because some answers only come when we fast.

Joshua was unaware of sin in the camp until he fasted and prayed. He knew that only the sovereign God could provide the answers he needed, so he bowed down in fasting. He was wise to seek the Lord rather than assemble a larger army and go back to battle.

Call to Action

We often fight harder for victory rather than seek God to tell us what's wrong in our lives. If the results of your battle do not match what you expect according to God's word, do not gather greater resources and go back out to battle. Call a fast; seek the Lord for answers. You may need to ask Him why you lost the battle when you completely trusted him to give you victory. God may reveal the sins in your life and give you strategies to overcome them as you fast.

So, as you fast and pray, consider whether you are losing battles you should be winning. Is there any sin in your camp? Do you depend on God wholeheartedly to fight your battles for you? Is there something in your life that you need to remove so that the favor of God can return to your life?

Take some time to seek the Lord concerning your situation and wait for Him to reveal the true nature of the problem. Once God reveals the pain, acknowledge and confess any hidden sins, repent, and accept God's forgiveness and favor. Refuse to accept defeat because the Sovereign God is fighting for you.

Promise: *"So I will restore to you the years that the swarming locust has eaten, The crawling locust, The consuming locust, and the chewing locust, My great army which I sent among you.* (Joel 2:25).

5

Gideon Fast

"Whenever the Israelites planted their crops, marauders from Midian, Amalek, and the people of the east would attack Israel, camping in the land and destroying crops as far away as Gaza. They left the Israelites with nothing to eat, taking all the sheep, goats, cattle, and donkeys. These enemy hordes, coming with their livestock and tents, were as thick as locusts; they arrived on droves of camels too numerous to count. And they stayed until the land was stripped bare. So Israel was reduced to starvation by the Midianites. Then the Israelites cried out to the Lord for help." (Judges 6:3-6).

At first glance, most people missed the Gideon fast because the Bible does not expressly state that Gideon or the Israelites were fasting. Most people are familiar with the story of Gideon threshing wheat in the wine press but seldom ever look beyond the fact that he was hiding it from the Midianites. It is only when you read into the back story of why Gideon was threshing wheat in the wine press that you get the understanding that there was some fasting and prayer taking place.

I received this understanding through revelation from the Holy

Spirit, and even so, I hesitated to write about Gideon's fast because I just didn't see where the Bible says he or the people was fasting. In fact, I left it completely out of the first manuscript of the book. As I grappled with the fact that the Bible doesn't expressly state that Gideon or the people were fasting, the Holy Spirit said to me, "Some things you can only receive by revelation." This gave me the confirmation to study Gideon's assignment through the lens of fasting.

When we read Gideon's story, we often focus on him threshing the wheat in the wine press. Seldom do we look beyond the wine press to observe what the other folks were doing while Gideon was in the wine press. So let us examine the backstory to find out more about this Gideon Fast. Judges 6:5-6 gives us the inside scoop on this forced fasting. It says, *"These enemy hordes, coming with their livestock and tents, were as thick as locusts; they arrived on droves of camels too numerous to count. And they stayed until the land was **stripped bare.** So Israel was **reduced to starvation** by the Midianites. Then the Israelites **cried out to the Lord** for help."*

Oppression of Israel

So the Children of Israel were under great oppression by the Midianites. The Lord permitted this oppression because they had turned away from Him and worshiped idols, namely Baal and Asherah, which was very displeasing to the Lord. The oppression was so severe that the Israelites could not even find food to eat. The Midianites destroyed their crops, stripped their land bare, and plundered their livestock, reducing Israel to starvation. So the people began to pray to the Lord for mercy.

When the Bible says the people cried out to the Lord, this meant they were fasting and weeping before the Lord, as was the case when Mordecai and the exiled Jews fasted and wept in the streets because of the death decree sent out against them.

By definition, fasting is abstaining from food. During Gideon's time, Israel was reduced to starvation, so they had no choice but to abstain from food. So this is not a traditional fast where people choose not to eat. They could not eat because they didn't have anything to eat. They cried out to the Lord in their distress, meaning they fasted and prayed to the Lord. Because Joel 2:12 says, *"Return to the Lord with all your heart, with fasting, weeping, and mourning."* Nothing to eat all day accompanied by praying and weeping before the Lord. Looks a lot like fasting now, doesn't it?

Most people only fast and pray when they are faced with calamity. When the problem becomes too big for us, it causes us to cry out to God. And the good news is God's ears are always open to the cries of His people even when they are doing wrong because He loves them and desires to help them to correct the error of their ways.

God Sent a Prophet

When the people cried out to God in their distress, *The Lord sent a prophet to the Israelites when they cried out to Him because of the Midianites. He said, "This is what the Lord, the God of Israel, says: I brought you up out of slavery in Egypt. I rescued you from the Egyptians and from all who oppressed you. I drove out your enemies and gave you their land. I told you, 'I am the Lord your God. You must not worship the gods of the Amorites, in whose land you now live.' But you have not listened to me."* (Judges 6:7-10). So again, we see fasting releasing the prophetic.

The people had done evil in the sight of God by building altars to Baal and Asherah, the gods of the Amorites. God warned them through the laws of Moses that He would punish them if they worshiped idols. So this Midianite's oppression was His method of causing them to see their sins.

We often do not see it when we sin, but God has a way of bringing us face to face with our sins. In this case, he told the prophet the tell them why they were in distress because they were oblivious to the cause of this severe oppression. How often have we found ourselves in distressing circumstances and asked God why? Have you ever considered that some of the painful things you face in life result from your wrong choices?

Mighty Man of Valor

While the people were crying out to God, Gideon was in a wine press, threshing out some wheat. Most likely, he was going to make some food for himself and his family, but the Angel of the Lord appeared and began speaking with him. As you read, pay close attention to their conversation because prayer is supposed to be a conversation between God and man. *"The Angel of the Lord appeared to him and said, "Mighty man of valor, the Lord is with you!" "Sir," Gideon replied, "if the Lord is with us, why has all this happened to us? And where are all the miracles our ancestors told us about? Didn't they say, 'The Lord brought us up out of Egypt'? But now the Lord has abandoned us and handed us over to the Midianites." Then the Lord turned to him and said, "Go with the strength you have and rescue Israel from the Midianites. I am sending you!"* (Judges 6:12-16 NLT).

You can see from Gideon's response that he was not impressed by an angelic visitation. Perhaps he didn't recognize him as an angel at first, or he was too focused on his problems to be concerned with an angel. So his response to the Angel was very sarcastic. *If God is with us, why is this happening to us?* Why are we reduced to starvation? In other words, he was saying listen here, I learned about the miracles that God has done through my forefathers, but I am not seeing any miracles now. All I see is starvation and oppression, so how can you say that God is with us?

From Gideon's response, you can tell that he didn't understand that the Lord was literally with him at that very moment. Gideon had a different idea of what *the Lord is with us* means. Think about it for a moment; God manifested himself to Gideon and told him I am right here with you, watching you threshing out that wheat in the wine press, but Gideon didn't recognize Him.

This makes me wonder, how many times have we missed God because He did not show up the way that we expected him to? Gideon was certainly not expecting God to show up sitting under a tree when Israel was starving. He was expecting God to do something about this terrible army that was oppressing Israel. How many times have we missed the day of our visitation because we are more focused on our problems than we are on hearing from God?

The Offering

The Lord was not offended by Gideon's sarcastic remarks. In fact, He attributed it to Gideon as strength. He told him, *"Go with the strength you have, and rescue Israel from the Midianites. I am sending you!"* (Judges 6:4). What strength was the angel talking about? Well, it took a lot of strength to backtalk an angel of the Lord, doesn't it? Gideon stood up to that angel and talked to him like a mighty man. So the Angel said alright then, mighty man, go with that same strength that causes you to feel so mighty that you can backtalk me. Go save Israel. You see, sometimes we can talk the talk, but it's a whole different story when it comes to walking out what we say.

When the Lord told him to use his strength to save Israel, Gideon protested, *"But Lord, how can I rescue Israel? My clan is the weakest in the whole tribe of Manasseh, and **I am the least** in my entire family!"* The Lord said to him, *"**I will be with you**. And you will destroy the Midianites as if you were fighting against one man."* (Judges 6:15-16). So now Gideon didn't feel so mighty as he realized the extent of what God was calling him to do. In other words, he said, Lord, do you realize this army is numberless? Lord, do you realize that I am only one person? I'm not that strong; I was only talking out of my mouth. I didn't mean it. Lord, I take back my words.

The Lord reassured Gideon, I'll go with you, but Gideon was not convinced. *"Gideon replied, "If you are truly going to help me, show me a sign to prove that it is really the Lord speaking to me."* (Judges 6:17). This is us all day long. We need fifty-nine confirmations before we step out in faith and do what God tells us to do.

Gideon decided to give an offering to the Lord. *"Gideon hurried home. He cooked a young goat, and with a basket of flour, he baked some bread without yeast. Then, carrying the meat in a basket and the broth in a pot, he brought them out and presented them to the angel under the great tree. The angel of God said to him, "Place the meat and the unleavened bread on this rock, and pour the broth over it." And Gideon did as he was told. Then the angel of the Lord touched the meat and bread with the tip of the staff in his hand, and fire flamed up from the rock and consumed all he had brought. And the angel of the Lord disappeared."* (Judges 6:19-21).

Let's think about this for a minute, there was starvation in the land, and people couldn't find food to eat. Gideon was hiding this wheat, but he cooked it with a young goat and offered it to this strange man under a tree. This meant that Gideon sacrificed the food he would prepare for his family. So not only were the people fasting and crying out to the Lord, but Gideon did his share of fasting too when he offered his meal to the Lord.

It was an unusual sacrificial offering since most offerings to the Lord are not usually offered in this manner. If Gideon knew he was really talking to the Lord, he would have made an altar to the Lord and prepared the offering in a different way.

However, the Lord accepted Gideon's offering and opened his eyes to understand that the Lord was really with him. *"When Gideon realized that it was the angel of the Lord, he cried out, "Oh, Sovereign Lord, I'm doomed! I have seen the angel of the Lord face to face!" "It is all right," the*

Lord replied. "Do not be afraid. You will not die." (Judges 6:22-23).

The thing about this offering that made it so acceptable to the Lord was Gideon gave his best offering to God during his time of need. This meant that Gideon trusted God more than the little wheat and meat he was about to eat.

After the Lord accepted the offering, He gave Gideon a series of divine directions and helped him to deliver His people Israel from the oppression of the Midianites.

The Battle Plan

First, the Lord instructs him to cut down the Baal altar and Asherah poles and create an altar to Yahweh. Then he sacrificed one of his father's bulls as a burnt offering to the Lord. This is significant before going out to battle because this was the thing that caused the oppression of Israel in the first place. Sometimes we come under enemy oppression because of some inner sins, but we often focus on the external enemy rather than the ones within us.

Internal issues usually cause the enemy to gain permission to oppress us. If we get rid of internal enemies such as unforgiveness, pride, resentment, envy, modern-day idol worship, careers, money, and people, God will give us victory over the external enemy. Anything we put in front of our relationship with God becomes an idol for us. So before Gideon went out to battle the external enemy, he dealt with the internal enemy.

As Gideon prepared to engage the vast army of Midianites, he sought further confirmation from God through a fleece and dew test before going into the battle. This is also very important because we should always seek confirmation from the Lord before entering into any spiritual warfare. Many times we rush into battle without consulting God for the battle plan. So this fleece and dew test gave Gideon confidence to gather the fighting men of Israel, but as he marched out to battle, the Lord told him that he had too many men.

The Lord helped Gideon select three hundred men to go with him in battle because He wanted Israel to know their victory. He wanted them to know that He was their God and that He fought their battles for them because He loved them. He wanted them to stop worshiping dead idols that could not fight for them.

The other interesting thing was the type of weapons that He gave them to fight with. *"He divided the 300 men into three groups and gave each man a **ram's horn** and a **clay jar** with a **torch** in it."* (Judges 7:16). At first glance these things do not look like weapons at all. So Gideon's army was stripped down to the bare minimum and given instruments that made no sense. Yet God gave them a miraculous victory over the Midianites.

This reminds us that the weapons of our warfare are not carnal, worldly weapons. Our defense is not in military might, such as guns, bombs, or missiles. Our weapons are the blood of the lamb, the testimony of Jesus, prayer, fasting, and faith in God. When these weapons are used according to God's directives, mighty victories are won.

Through these peculiar instruments, the Lord gave Gideon and his three hundred men victory over the vast Midianites' vast army. *"When the 300 Israelites blew their rams' horns and broke their clay jars, the Lord caused the warriors in the Midianites camp to fight against each other with their swords. Those who were not killed fled...."* (Judges 7:22)

So God heard the prayers of His people and sent a prophet to tell them why they were oppressed. Then, He sent a deliverer to fight for them and free them from oppression. As you read this story, you cannot help but wonder what it is about human beings that cause God to respond to their cries. Isaiah 54:7 gives us good insight as to why God answers us even when we sin against him, *"For a brief moment I abandoned you, but with great compassion, I will take you back."* God's great love and compassion for His people caused Him to respond to their cries continually. God's love and compassion are the same for us today. Whenever you feel afraid or oppressed, you can cry out to Him; he hears even our faintest cries and takes delight in showing us mercy.

Call to Action

Sometimes the trials we experience are an indication of how far we are from God. Without the oppression of the Midianites, the Israelites wouldn't cry out to God because they wouldn't see the error of their ways. So this oppression was a chastening from the Lord. And we all know that no chastening is pleasant at the time, but it yields goodness and righteousness in the end.

So as you fast and pray today, if you are experiencing difficult circumstances in your life, maybe it's time to cry out to God as the Israelites did. Cry out to God with a Holy expectation that He will hear and answer your prayers. And if He sends a prophet to warn you of some sin in your life. Repent and return to God with all of your heart.

Also, be mindful of the things operating as idols in your life. Nowadays, people are not walking around with wooden images as idols, but there are many things that they idolize, such as money, possessions, and other people, especially people in positions of power. Be mindful that anything you put in place of God is an idol to you. And remember that God is a Jealous God. He will not share His glory with idols.

Promise: *"In a burst of anger, I turned my face away for a little while. But with everlasting love, I will have compassion on you," says the Lord, your Redeemer."* (Isaiah 54:8)

6

Hannah's Fast

"Year after year it was the same, Peninnah would taunt Hannah as they went to the Tabernacle. Hannah would be reduced to tears and would not even eat. "Why are you crying, Hannah?" Elkanah would ask. "Why aren't you eating? Why be downhearted just because you have no children? You have me, isn't that better than having ten sons?" (1 Samuel 1:7-8).

This is another beautiful example of the power of fasting and prayer. Hannah was in great anguish in her soul because she couldn't have children. Instead of blaming God or becoming angry at God, she turned to Him in fasting and prayer.

Many of us have gone through seasons of barrenness, where nothing seems to work in our lives. It seems like everything you tried turns out to be a failure. You kind of live your life going from failure to failure, and if that's not bad enough, others mock you.

This was exactly where Hannah was; year after year, she would try but fail to conceive, and her counterpart Peninnah would continue bearing children. In her distress, she decided not to eat; in other words, she chose to fast and pray because she knew of the power of prayer and fasting. Let's go find out how she successfully touched the Heart of God.

Hannah's Vow

Hannah realized that she was barren, and so she began to pray to the Lord about it, but nothing happened. Then she became sad because her prayers were not answered, and she felt like God had forgotten her, so she decided to add some fasting to the prayer. Still, nothing happened, so she added something else to her prayer and fasting. She decided to make a vow to Lord. *"Hannah was in deep anguish, crying bitterly as she prayed to the Lord. And* **she made this vow:** *"O Lord of Heaven's Armies, if you will look upon my sorrow and answer my prayer and give me a son, then I will give him back to you. He will be yours for his entire lifetime, and as a sign that he has been dedicated to the Lord, his* **hair will never be cut.***"* (1 Samuel 1:10-11). This was no ordinary vow; it was a Nazirite vow. She took a Nazirite vow to consecrate herself and her child to the Lord.

Nazirites refrain from drinking strong drinks, cutting their hair, or handling dead or unclean objects. *"As long as they are bound by their Nazirite vow, they are not allowed to eat or drink anything that comes from a grapevine—not even the grape seeds or skins. "They must never cut their hair throughout the time of their vow, for they are holy and set apart to the Lord. Until the time of their vow has been fulfilled, they must let their hair grow long. And they must not go near a dead body during the entire period of their vow to the Lord."* (Numbers 6:4-6). Such were the laws that governed Nazirite vows since Moses' time.

Hannah must have also known about Samson and his parents, who were chosen to give birth to a Nazirite, because her vow is very similar to what the angel told Manoah's wife, *"Even though you have been unable to have children, you will soon become pregnant and give birth to a son. So be careful; you must not drink wine or any other alcoholic drink nor eat any forbidden food. You will become pregnant and give birth to a son, and his hair must never be cut, for he will be dedicated to God as a Nazirite from birth. He will begin to rescue Israel from the Philistines."* (Judges

13:3-5). So Hannah refrained from drinking any strong drinks, and she promised that if God gave her a child, his hair would not be cut.

Hannah's Prayer

When Hannah's family went to the temple to worship, it was customary for them to offer sacrifices and feast at the temple, but Hannah refused to eat. She kept on fasting and praying. Eli, the priest, noticed she was speaking, but no sound was coming from her mouth, so he assumed she was drunk. He even reprimanded her, *"Must you come here drunk?" he demanded. "Throw away your wine!"* (1 Samuel 1:14). It is ironic that the priest would even assume such a thing about someone who gave up wine to be consecrated to God. It's typical of the enemy to accuse you of things you're not guilty of.

I admire Hannah's response because she did not become offended by Eli's accusations. *She simply replied, "Oh no, sir!* **I haven't been drinking wine or drinking any strong drink.** *But I was very discouraged, and I was pouring out my heart to the Lord. Don't think I am a wicked woman! For I have been praying out of great anguish and sorrow."* And then observe how the priest responded to her and how it changed her countenance. *Eli said, "In that case, go in peace! May the God of Israel grant the request you have asked of him." "Oh, thank you, sir!" she exclaimed. Then she went back and* **began to eat again, and she was no longer sad."** (1 Samuel 1:15-18).

She believed the prophetic utterance of the priest. Something in Eli's response caused Hannah to know that her request had been granted. Her sadness left her, so she broke her fast and began eating again because she knew God heard her prayers and the answer was coming. She went home with her husband, and shortly thereafter, she conceived and gave birth to Samuel. But the story doesn't end there because it's one thing to make a vow but a whole different thing to keep.

Fulfill your vows

So after Hannah gave birth to the child, I can imagine how difficult it must have been for her to give up her only child, but that was the promise she made to God. The people who made Nazirite vows to God were required to follow the laws of the Nazirites, which were to bring specific offerings to the Lord and other offerings if they could afford them. They had to do what they promised in order to fulfill their Nazarite vow. (See Numbers 6:21). This law was there to help the people keep their end of the vow to God because Moses knew that temptations and trials would always come to make it difficult to keep the vow. Hannah was fully aware of what it meant to fulfill her Nazarite vow, but it was difficult to keep that vow.

> *"The next year Elkanah and his family went on their annual trip to offer a sacrifice to the Lord and to keep his vow, but Hannah did not go. She told her husband, "Wait until the boy is weaned. Then I will take him to the Tabernacle and permanently leave him there with the Lord." "Whatever you think is best," Elkanah agreed.* ***"Stay here for now, and may the Lord help you keep your promise."*** *So she stayed home and nursed the boy until he was weaned. (1 Samuel 1:21-23).*

It is important to note that her husband prayed that the Lord would help her keep her promise. Hannah's husband was the closest to her, so he would recognize how difficult it was for her to keep such a promise. She must have been so overjoyed at the prospect of giving birth and so in love with her baby that he could not imagine her giving up such an important part of her life. Even though it wasn't mentioned, Elkanah must have felt the same way Hannah did, even though it wasn't mentioned. He wholeheartedly supported his wife's decision because he understood what it means to honor their vows to the Lord.

So although it was difficult, they consecrated young Samuel to the temple.

> *When the child was weaned, Hannah took him to the Tabernacle in Shiloh. They brought along a **three-year-old bull for the sacrifice** and **a basket of flour and some wine**. After sacrificing the bull, they brought the boy to Eli. "Sir, do you remember me?" Hannah asked. "I am the very woman who stood here several years ago praying to the Lord. I asked the Lord to give me this boy, and he granted my request. **Now I am giving him to the Lord, and he will belong to the Lord his whole life."** And they worshiped the Lord there."* (1 Samuel 1:24-28).

What an amazing, beautiful fulfillment of a vow. In addition to giving the child to the Lord, Hannah brought a three-year-old bull, a basket of flour, and some wine. So Hannah fulfilled her promise to the Lord and followed the Nazirite as was written by Moses. Although it was difficult, Hannah gave the only child she had to the Lord, and she was happy to do it because she worshiped the Lord after giving up the children. *"Then Hannah prayed: "My heart rejoices in the Lord! The Lord has made me strong. Now I have an answer for my enemies; I rejoice because you rescued me. No one is holy like the Lord! There is no one besides you; there is no Rock like our God."* (1 Samuel 2:1-2). She didn't go home in distress, wondering if she had done the right thing. She wholeheartedly gave her gift to the Lord and rejoiced while doing so.

Hannah was a cheerful giver; she kept her promise to the Lord, and because she kept her promise, the Lord rewarded her greatly. She sowed one child and reaped a harvest of children. Each year when they visited the temple, *"Eli would bless Elkanah and his wife before they returned home and say, "May the Lord give you other children to take the place of this one she gave to the Lord." And the Lord blessed Hannah, and she* *conceived and gave **birth to three sons and two daughters**. Meanwhile, Samuel grew up in the presence of the Lord."* (1 Samuel 2:20-21). And you know the rest of the story of how Samuel faithfully served the Lord as a Nazirite priest, prophet, and judge of Israel all of his life.

Call to Action

So, as you continue on your fasting journey, consider what are some of the things in your life that have been a source of failure or bareness. It could be your health, finances, career achievements, or accomplishments, or you are like Hannah and desire to conceive, but it just seems like nothing is working. Everything you try just results in failure. Maybe you prayed, fasted, read the word, and stood in faith, but nothing is happening. Have you tried making a vow to the Lord? Ask Him to show you what He wants you to do on earth and come into an agreement or covenant with God to do it.

In Hannah's case, God wanted a Nazirite, and Hannah wanted a son. When Hannah came into a covenant agreement, they both got what they wanted. Samuel's life tremendously impacted the Israelites and the world today. And it only happened because one woman chose to fast and pray.

So as you fast and pray today, ask God to reveal his will for your life. Consider how your desire aligns with God's will and desires for your life. Once you understand what God wants from you, commit to doing whatever it takes to get it done.

Promise *If you fully obey the Lord your God and carefully follow all his commands I give you today, the Lord your God will set you high above all the nations on earth.* (Deuteronomy 28:1)

7

David Fast

"David pleaded with God for the child. He fasted and spent the nights lying in sackcloth on the ground. The elders of his household stood beside him to get him up from the ground, but he refused and would not eat any food with them. On the seventh day, the child died. David's attendants were afraid to tell him that the child was dead, for they thought, "while the child was still living, he wouldn't listen to us when we spoke to him. How can we now tell him the child is dead? He may do something desperate." (2 Samuel 12:16-23)

The loss of a child is one of the most traumatic experiences in a person's life. It is not something anyone wants to experience. When King David received a prophetic message that his newborn son was going to die, he immediately began fasting and praying. After humbling himself in sackcloth and ashes and pleading with God for seven days, the child died. At first glance, it may seem that God is unfair or uncaring because the King fasted and repented, but God did not spare the child. Why would God allow such a terrible tragedy? Let's explore David's fast to understand how to pray when we receive a negative prophetic word.

David's Actions

This tragic situation began when King David committed adultery with Bathsheba and murdered her husband, Uriah. Bathsheba became his wife, and she became pregnant and gave birth to a son. The Lord sent the prophet Nathan to warn David that judgment was coming to his house. *David said to Nathan, "I have sinned against the Lord." Nathan replied, "The Lord has taken away your sin. You are not going to die." "But because by doing this, you have shown utter contempt for the Lord, the son born to you will die."* (2 Samuel 12: 13-14). David immediately confessed his sins when the prophet confronted him. *"I have sinned against the Lord."* are some of the hardest words to utter, especially when you are the king of Israel, and everyone looks up to you.

This is remarkable because most people make excuses and cover up their sins rather than admit their mistakes. When his predecessor, King Saul, sinned, God sent the prophet Samuel to warn him, and although he acknowledged his sins, he did not repent. Instead, he told Samuel, *"I have sinned. But please honor me before the elders of my people and before Israel; come back with me, so that I may worship the Lord your God."* (I Samuel 15:30). King Saul was more concerned with his self-image than he was concerned with pleasing God. So when confronted by the prophet, he tried to cover up his sins instead of repenting as David did. When confronted with your sins, the best thing to do is to humble yourself, acknowledge your faults, and ask God for mercy because you cannot receive forgiveness if you do not acknowledge your sins and repent. When we hide our sins, we are at risk of continuing to sin or invoking the worst punishment on ourselves, as King Saul did. Knowing this, David immediately began fasting and praying after the prophet left.

David's Prayer

Observe that David's fast was initiated by the prophetic word he received. Because God delights in showing mercy, He often sends prophets to give us instructions or warnings that prompt us to fast and pray. Although God's prophetic warnings are not always pleasant, they are His mercy in disguise because He really wants to spare people from judgment.

So David received the prophetic warning as an invitation to fast and pray. We can learn from David's prayer in Psalm 51 how to deal with unpleasant prophetic words. He prayed, *"Have mercy on me, O God, according to your unfailing love; according to your great compassion, blot out my transgressions. Wash away all my iniquity and cleanse me from my sin. For I know my transgressions and my sin is always before me. Against you, you only, have I sinned and done what is evil in your sight, so you are right in your verdict and justified when you judge.* (Psalms 51:1-4). David first acknowledged and confessed that he sinned against God and that the Lord's judgment was righteous. He knew that God's love and compassion for humanity is great, so he pleaded with God for mercy.

Then, he asked the Lord, *"Purify me with hyssop, and I will be clean; wash me, and I will be whiter than snow.* (Psalms 51:7). David knew that only the Lord could forgive him and cleanse him of the evil he had done. Next, he asked the Lord, *"Create in me a pure heart, O God, and renew a steadfast spirit within me."* (Psalms 51:10). The prophetic word he received opened his eyes to the evil in his heart, and David wanted his heart to be purified of this evil.

Many times we recognize these things about ourselves, but we don't pray as David did. When we know we have done something wrong, asking God to cleanse our hearts and renew our spirits is important. The cleansing of our hearts refers to deliverance from the evil spirits that cause us to sin. If God does not cleanse our hearts, we will continue to sin. Therefore, it's important to seek deliverance from the Lord.

David continued to pray, *"Do not cast me from your presence or take your*

Holy Spirit from me." (Psalms 51:11). This was incredibly important to David because he saw what happened to King Saul when the Holy Spirit was taken from him. He was the one who played the harp for King Saul to get relief from the evil spirit that troubled him, and David wanted no part of that. (See I Samuel 16).

David also promised the Lord that if He forgave him of his sins, *"I will teach transgressors Your ways, and sinners will return to You.* It's hard to believe that any good can come out of evil, but the most noteworthy benefit of sin is to learn from it and to teach others the lessons you learned. Unfortunately, many people never learned their lessons, so they continue sinning without reaping the benefits of their mistakes. David's example still teaches us today about the mercy of God and how to repent and return to God when we sin.

David understood that sin is a matter of the heart and no amount of burnt sacrifice would take his sins away, so he prayed, *"You do not delight in sacrifice, or I would bring it; You take no pleasure in burnt offerings. The sacrifices of God are a broken spirit, a broken and a contrite heart, O God, You will not despise. (Psalm 51:16-17).* He would offer it to God if a burnt offering or a sacrifice could make this right. However, he knew the Lord had no delight in burnt offerings, so he offered God the only thing he could, his broken heart. He knew God would not reject a heart that was truly broken and remorseful.

Likewise, when we sin, no amount of money or service can make up for the wrong we have done. The only thing God wants from us is sincere sorrow and repentance from our sins. David's sorrow was sincere, and his pleas were heartfelt, and God forgave his sins, but his still baby died. Let's find out why.

David's Response

Upon hearing that the child had died, he stopped praying. *"David noticed his attendants* were *whispering among themselves, and he realized the child was dead. "Is the child dead?" he asked. "Yes," they replied, "he is dead." Then David got up from the ground. After he had washed, put on lotions, and changed his clothes, he went into the house of the Lord and worshiped. Then he went to his own house, and at his request, they served him food, and he ate. His attendants asked him, "Why are you acting this way? While the child was alive, you fasted and wept, but now that the child is dead, you get up and eat!" He answered, "While the child was still alive, I fasted and wept. I thought, 'Who knows? The Lord may be gracious to me and let the child live.' But now that he is dead, why should I go on fasting? Can I bring him back again? I will go to him, but he will not return to me."* (2 Samuel 12:19-23 NIV)

The newborn child took David's punishment because the law of Israel in those days was a life for a life. David deserves death because he murdered Uriah; in his own words, *any man who would do such a thing deserves to die.* (2 Samuel 12:5). Although he deserved death, the Lord allowed him to live but took the life of his newborn child.

The death of the child was still God's mercy in disguise because God punished David by taking the child. However, the child's innocence was preserved because he took him back to heaven. So David's life was spared, and the child went to live with God in heaven. You could say this was a win-win situation for David, considering he deserves death.

When Babies Die

Like David, many people have experienced the tragic loss of a child, whether it's through miscarriage, abortion, or death after they were born. At some point, the question becomes, where do babies go when they die? I have heard many stories about people who went to heaven and actually saw a nursery and children playing in heaven. One lady said that God revealed to her that there are no babies or children in hell because babies go back to heaven when they die.

This is conceivable to me because Jesus alluded to this in Matthew

18:10 when he said, *"See that you do not despise one of these little ones. For I tell you that their angels in heaven always see the face of my Father in heaven."* Well, how do their angels see the face of God? I believe that this is referring to when children die. Some may refute it and say that Jesus is referring to children's guardian angels, but that does not compute. Jesus also said in Matthew 18:3, *unless you change and become like little children, you will never enter the kingdom of heaven."*

The takeaway from this verse is that children do enter heaven. Jesus even followed up later in Matthew 19:14 by saying, *"Allow the children to come to me. Don't stop them! For the Kingdom of Heaven belongs to those, who are like these children."*

Some people say the age of innocence is thirteen according to Jewish customs, but we don't really know for certain because the Bible doesn't give us any specific information concerning the matter. My belief is that it has more to do with spiritual maturity than the child's age, but again, we don't know for certain. So when David said, *I will go to the child, but he will not return to me.* This meant that David knew the child was in heaven.

David understood from the previous fasting that sometimes God doesn't give us what we pray for. He said in Psalm 35: 13, *I denied myself by fasting for them, but my prayers returned unanswered."* He understood that even God's 'no' was filled with grace and mercy. So David accepted his punishment as God's sovereign will and repented for his sins. The beautiful end to the story is that God gave David another child who later became the famous King Solomon, whom God used to build His temple.

Call to Action

David's fast began with a negative prophetic word from the Lord, which drove him to fast and pray. He did not get the desired result: the newborn child's life. Although his fasting successfully touched the heart of God, the child died, but God forgave him for his sins and gave him another son.

God will not always grant us the desires of our hearts when we pray because His ways are higher than our ways, so we should humble ourselves as David did and accept God's "no." Could it be that sometimes when God tells us no, even in the most painful situations in our lives, it is His mercy in disguise? David deserves death for what he did, but God, in His mercy, chose a different form of punishment for him.

As you fast and pray today, consider some things you have done in your past. How are they affecting your present situation? How are they affecting your children? Has God given you a prophetic word that brought your face-to-face with your past? Are you prepared to accept a "no" answer to your fasting and prayer requests?

I encourage you to pray and ask the Lord to help you discern when He says "no" and give you the grace and humility to accept it. The sooner you can accept God's "no," the quicker you will receive your breakthrough.

Promise: *"Then you shall know that I am in the midst of Israel: I am the Lord your God, And there is no other. My people shall never be put to shame."* (Joel 2:27).

8

Elijah Fast

"The angel of the Lord came back a second time and touched him and said, "Get up and eat, for the journey is too much for you." So he got up and ate and drank. Strengthened by that food, he traveled forty days and forty nights until he reached Horeb, the mountain of God." (1 Kings 19:7-8)

Have you ever felt you have done everything God told you to do, but the results you received were not exactly what you hoped for? Elijah did everything God told him to do. He boldly prophesied to King Ahab that there would be no rain, and it didn't rain for three and a half years. He killed all the false prophets in the presence of the king and all the people of Israel. Then he prayed for rain, and it rained; he outran Ahab's chariot. Then, Jezebel threatened to kill him, and Elijah ran away, lay down under a tree in the wilderness, and prayed for God to take his life. How did God respond to such a prayer?

Take My Life

To understand what was happening with Elijah, we must understand what Elijah was expecting after accomplishing all the things God told him to do. Elijah expected Jezebel would finally understand that

Israel's God was the real God. Elijah expected Jezebel to repent and accept the God of Israel as the people did on Mount Carmel, but instead, she threatened to kill him.

The Bible says Elijah was afraid and ran for his life. This puzzled me for a while because Elijah was not afraid when he stood before the king and prophesied that there would be no rain. He was not afraid when he told the king, *"Now summon all Israel to join me at Mount Carmel, along with the 450 prophets of Baal and the 400 prophets of Asherah who are supported by Jezebel."* (I Kings 18:19 NLT). He was not afraid to slay all 850 false prophets of Baal and Asherah. So why was Elijah afraid?

All the miraculous things that Elijah did were under the direction of the Holy Spirit. But when Jezebel threatened him, Elijah was afraid because he didn't have any further directions from the Lord. He didn't know how to handle this threat. So this drove him on a supernatural fast. He was not really planning to fast; all he wanted was to die. Elijah went into the wilderness, lay under a broom tree, and prayed, *"Take my life. I'm no better than my fathers."* The interesting thing about God's response to Elijah was that He didn't scold Elijah; He did not even answer Elijah's complaint. The Lord responded by feeding him some 'angel food.'

The Journey

Sometimes God will answer our prayers in ways that make no sense until we obey by faith. Elijah was lying under this broom tree, praying to die, and the Lord sent an angel to feed him. I can imagine Elijah asking God, why would you send an angel to feed me? I am praying for you to take my life. So when the angel fed him the first time, he went back to sleep. Then the angel came and fed him a second time and told him, *"Eat, for the journey is too much for you."* Elijah knew nothing about a journey or where he was going. He was unprepared for the journey, had no bags, food, or water, and was in the wilderness.

When the angel told him about the journey, I imagined Elijah's spirit came alive. Suddenly, there was something to live for. Elijah got up, ate, drank, *and was strengthened by that food; he traveled forty days and forty nights.* He didn't know where God was leading him but knew he could no longer stay under the broom tree. Elijah journeyed through the wilderness from Beersheba to Mount Horeb without food or water. This journey was physically impossible because of the hills and valleys and the windy and dry climate in that region, which made it difficult to traverse that terrain on foot. A journey of this nature requires endurance and complete trust in God. Elijah trusts that wherever his feet took him is exactly where God wanted him to go.

Supernatural Fast

Elijah was fasting when he lay under the broom tree because he wanted to hear from God. He didn't eat or drink until the angel fed him. He had reached his limit, but fasting has a way of taking us beyond our natural limitations. Elijah had no hope of doing anything else in Israel because, after all the miracles God had done, Jezebel refused to repent. Elijah gave up fighting to save Israel from the wrath of God. He was saying what some pastors are saying today; I'm done with the ministry, God! After all, I have done for these people; they are trying to kill me. Lord, just take my life. Please understand this Elijah was not suicidal. He was not going to harm himself, but he wanted to go and be with the Lord.

Instead of taking his life, God invited Elijah to go on a fasting journey through the wilderness. Can you imagine hiking over mountains and valleys with no food or water for forty days? Elijah must have become tired, stopped, and slept in some caves along the way, but he kept going. The food that the angel fed him supernaturally sustained him for forty days.

Elijah's fast was supernatural because it's physically impossible to survive that long in the wilderness without food or water. Moses and Jesus were the only other two people who fasted supernaturally.

Mountain of God

Of all the places Elijah could end up, he ended up on Mount Horeb, the mountain of God. He found a cave and spent the night with a hard rock for a bed, talk about a hard rock hotel. Can you imagine being on a forty-day journey with no food or water and finally reaching your destination, but it is a dark, dusty cave? There was no welcome party, no-cooked meal, warm baths, or clean sheets. Sometimes God calls us to go through wilderness seasons, which causes us to end up in a cave of solitude.

A cave represents times in your life when you are alone with God. No one can help you but God. No one understands what you are going through but God. You may not end up in a literal cave like Elijah, but somewhere in your mind and spirit, you are alone.

Can you imagine Elijah saying, Lord, you mean to tell me you let me leave my broom tree for a cave? God, I had to walk through the wilderness for forty days and forty nights, and this is the best you could offer, a cave? The prophet didn't question it, he just lay down to sleep, but as he slept in the cave, strange things happened.

First, the Lord spoke to him. This is what he wanted, right? He wanted to hear from the Lord! He wanted to know what God was going to do about idolatry in the nation. God didn't come with some sweet, comforting words like, my wonderful servant, you did great, let me soothe your pain. God asked, *"What are you doing here, Elijah?"* Elijah replied, *"I have been very zealous for the Lord God Almighty. The Israelites have rejected your covenant, torn down your altars, and put your prophets to death with the sword. I am the only one left, and now they are trying to kill me, too."* (1 Kings 19:10).

As Elijah conversed with God, something crazy happened. A

whirlwind ripped through the mountain, shredding rocks to pieces. An earthquake shook the mountain, and fire blazed on the mountainside, and then the Lord spoke in a still, small voice. *So it was when Elijah heard it that he wrapped his face in his mantle and went out and stood at the entrance of the cave. Suddenly a voice came to him, and said, "What are you doing here, Elijah?* (1 Kings 19:13). Elijah's forty-day fasting journey led him straight to the heart of God. In response to Elijah's passionate devotion, God revealed His prophetic plans to him and showed him His glory.

The Plan

The first thing the Lord said to him was, *"Go back the way you came and go to the Desert of Damascus. When you get there, anoint Hazael king over Aram. Also, anoint Jehu, son of Nimshi, king over Israel, and anoint Elisha's son of Shaphat, from Abel Meholah to succeed you as a prophet. Jehu will put to death any who escape the sword of Hazael, and Elisha will put to death any who escape the sword of Jehu.* (I Kings 19: 15-17). The first thing the Lord said to Elijah was, *'go back the way you came.'* Elijah had to go back through the wilderness, probably another forty-day journey with no food or water. The only other person who fasted for eighty consecutive days was Moses, and he did it on this same mountain in the presence of God. So Both Elijah and Moses were in the presence of the Lord as they fasted for eighty days, and they both received prophetic instructions from God.

The next thing God revealed was the next king of Israel, King of Aram, and the prophet that would replace Elijah. Then God revealed to Elijah that He was going to bring judgment by the sword. King Hazael, King Jehu, and Prophet Elisha were anointed to bring judgment by the sword.

God also told Elijah that he was not the only one left. *"Yet I reserve seven thousand in Israel, all whose knees have not bowed down to Baal and whose mouths have not kissed him."* (1 Kings 19:18). Thus, God showed Elijah his prophetic plans for Israel and corrected him for believing he was Israel's only prophet.

Call to Action

Elijah's fast began with prophetic instructions and ended with prophetic instructions. During Elijah's 40-day fast, he received a prophetic word that spans decades of Israel's history. The only conclusion to draw here is that fasting releases the prophetic, just as the prophetic causes us to fast. One man's fast changed the course of an entire nation.

As you fast today, remember some prophecies only come through fasting and prayer. You may need to lay down under a broom tree in your wilderness and wait on God's instructions.

When we have no word from God, we have nothing to guide us, and we will quickly come to the end of our human efforts. The Lord says, come to me all who labor and are heavy laden, and I will give you rest.

If you are discouraged, tired, and weary, God will send an angel to feed your soul with the bread of heaven. Completely trust God to sustain you on your fasting journey because He is able to preserve you, even in the wilderness. However, do not fast as Elijah did unless God graced you with a supernatural encounter. Maintain your zeal for God, and you will successfully touch the heart of God. Listen for his prophetic instructions to you. Ask Him to release his divine plans to you as you fast.

Promise: *"The Lord replied to them: "I am sending you grain, new wine, and olive oil, enough to satisfy you fully; never again will I make you an object of scorn to the nations."* (Joel 2:19)

9

Widows Fast

"But Elijah said to her, "Don't be afraid! Go ahead and do just what you've said, but make a little bread for me first. Then use what's left to prepare a meal for yourself and your son. For this is what the Lord, the God of Israel, says: There will always be flour and olive oil left in your containers until the time when the Lord sends the rain, and the crops grow again!" So she did as Elijah said, and she and Elijah and her family continued to eat for many days." (1 Kings 17:13-15).

When we talk about the widow's fast, most people think of Anna fasting in the temple, but there was a widow's fast way before Anna's time. This fasting is not expressly stated as a fast, and most people would not even think of this as a fast. However, if we pause long enough to observe what is happening here, we will understand that the widow woman of Zarephath was in a fasting situation. It was not her intention to fast, but there was a famine in the land, so she could not eat as she normally would. Most likely, she rationed out her meals to one meal per day because she was in a famine. So most likely, she waited all day to eat this last meal, and to complicate matters, just when she was about to make her dinner, a strange little man appeared and asked that she give him a meal first. Consequently, she had to wait even longer to eat her food. And remember that was her last meal so she was about to give away the last thing she had to eat. Every story has a back story, so let's get into it to find out what we can learn.

The Brook dried up

The story began long before Elijah arrived at the widow's house in Zarephath. You could even say that Elijah was partially responsible for this famine because he told King Ahab that there would be no rain in Israel until he said so. Then the Lord told him to go hide by the brook Cherith, but one day the brook dried up, and the Lord told him to go to Zarephath because he had commanded a widow woman to feed him.

This dried-up brook was a prophecy being fulfilled because idol worshiping and witchcraft had reached their peak in Israel. Jezebel had set up Baal and Asherah altars, and idol worshipping was the national religion of the day. So God sent the prophet to warn them that there would be no rain. This is what God told them would happen way back in Moses' day. Deuteronomy 11:16-17 *says, Be careful, or you will be enticed to turn away and worship other gods and bow down to them. Then the Lord's anger will burn against you, and he will shut up the heavens so that it will not rain and the ground will yield no produce, and you will soon perish from the good land the Lord is giving you.* We see Elijah many years later, prophesying that there would be no rain in Israel until the Lord said so, and it did not rain. Therefore, it's logical that the brook would dry up.

It is interesting to note that God spoke after the book dried up. Sometimes we cannot hear the voice of God over the babbling brook. Your dry brook is only serving to notify that God is speaking. God had to dry up that brook because you had become too engrossed in it. You fell in love with the brook and left your first love. The things of

God have become the second place in your life because you are busy attending to the brook. You are too busy; you don't have time to read your bible and pray because you are busy by the brook. Remember how you end up at the brook? It was God who sent you there. The brook represents the job you prayed for, and God gave you, but now it has caused God to become second place in your life.

The Road to Zeraphath

When the brook dries up, it is not time to sit and lament over it. It's time to prepare for what's next. It's time to get ready to go to the Zarephath. After the book dried up, go to Elijah go to Zarephath. Some scholars say that Zarephath was *about 100 miles away* from the brook. So Elijah had to leave the comfort of the brook and walk for days to reach Zarephath. It was a long journey without food or water, so I imagine he became tired and weary along the way. There were probably hills and valleys along the road to Zarephath, and the road was probably hot and dusty.

Sometimes it might take a while to get to your next job, meal, or rest stop. You may have to go through a long and winding process to get there. Many times along the way, you may ask God, why is it taking so long? You may even say Lord, I am tired. I have done everything you told me to do, but there seems to be no rest in sight. The children are still acting up, your marriage is still not fixed, and no new opportunities are on the horizon. There is just one problem after another, and you may even ask the Lord, will I ever get a break? God, I'm doing everything you told me to do. I didn't expect it to be so difficult. God, my heart is willing, but my flesh is weak! But Elijah did not complain. He got up and headed out to Zarephath.

The Widow Woman

Elijah finally managed to reach Zarephath, exhausted and hungry.

Since a raven fed him by the brook, it is unlikely he would have been able to save enough food to take with him. The first person he met at Zarephath was a widow woman, gathering sticks to make her last meal. Elijah was so thirsty that he first asked for a cup of water. As she went to get the water, he also told her to bring me some bread. She said I only have enough for me and my son to eat and then die.

It seemed like her brook had dried up too! What was God doing sending the prophet to someone who could barely provide for themselves? So, both the prophet and the woman had a crisis. At this point, many of us begin to question the Lord. Lord, I thought you said you commanded this widow woman to feed me? She seemed surprised to see me. What's up with this Lord? You didn't tell her I was coming? And Lord, she doesn't have enough for herself. But the Prophet had confidence in the Lord. So he told her don't be afraid, do as I have said, make me a meal first. The Lord God of Israel says, *'The jar of flour will not be exhausted, and the jug of oil will not run dry until the day the LORD sends rain upon the face of the earth.'* (I Kings 17:14).

She probably thought this man must be crazy, but she obeyed. You know this took some faith because it was her last meal, and her child depended on her to feed him. But this is one of the classic requirements of God's chosen fast in Isaiah 58. God says, *"Share your food with the hungry, and give shelter to the homeless. Give clothes to those who need them and do not hide from relatives who need your help."* (Isaiah 58:7).

The Prophets Reward

The widow woman activated her faith when she believed the prophet and did what he requested. She believed the prophet and received the prophet's reward because her jar of flour didn't go empty, and her jug of oil did not run dry. Her miracle was locked up in her obedience. Her Miracle began with a dried-up brook. The brook had to dry up so Elijah could be the answer to this woman's needs.

But the miracles didn't end there. The Bible said that sometimes later, the woman's son died. The woman cried out to the prophet, why did you bring this tragedy on me? **The prophet cried out to God,** *"O LORD my God,* **have You also brought tragedy** *on this widow who has opened her home to me by causing her son to die?" Then he stretched himself out over the child three times and cried out to the LORD,* **"O LORD my God, please let this boy's life return to him!"** (I Kings 17:19-21). Therefore, Elijah questioned God about that dried-up brook because that word *also* denotes in addition to something. So Elijah was saying, in addition to drying up the brook, you are going to cause this widow woman's son to die? Elijah was like oh no!!! uh-uh!! It's one thing for you a dry up a brook God, but to cause the widow's child to die! Ok, God, we got some talking to do; let's get behind closed doors.

It is sometimes necessary to question the Lord about your circumstance; otherwise, how will you know God's will? Listen, it's time to talk to God about that thing in the prayer closet! So, the woman cried out to the prophet, and the prophet cried out to God. God, listen to the prophet, and the child's life returned to him. The woman said *now I know that you are truly a man of God and that you speak the truth.* The woman and her son were facing death, so God caused Elijah's brook to dry up so he could help them fight the famine. Why would God do that? Well, I suspect that this woman was praying through her famine, and God used the prophet to answer her prayers.

Call to Action

Be careful not to allow the brook to take the place of God in your life. God will dry up anything that tries to take His place. Our total dependency should be on God and no one else or anything else. The brook represents that thing that we lean on for comfort. It represents our job, ministry, family, career, finances, etc.

God could have kept the brook running just like he kept the flour and the oil from running out, but God needed Elijah to go to Zarephath. So your dried-up brook may be the answer to someone else miracle? What is it that has dried up in your life? Could it be that's it because someone's miracle is depending on you? Which one are you? Are you Elijah or the widow woman? They both had to obey God. Elijah had to leave the brook. The woman had the make the meal for the prophet first.

story

Your dried-up brook is the answer to someone's prayer. *Your dried-up brook is the key to someone else's miracle.* The widow woman only had one last meal in her barrel. She and her son were going to eat it and then die. *She needed the prophetic word to keep that jar of flour and jug of oil full.* When her son died, she needed the prophet to intercede. You might just be one prophetic word away from your miracle. You may need to receive a prophet in the name of a prophet.

So, as you fast and pray today, consider which position you are in. Are you in the prophet's position that had to leave the brook, or are you the widow woman that needs the prophet? What is God telling you to walk away from? Are you willing to walk away from it? Are you willing to share your food with the hungry?

Promise: *God is not a man, so he does not lie. He is not human, so he does not change his mind. Has he ever spoken and failed to act? Has he ever promised and not carried it through? I received a command to bless; God has blessed, and I cannot reverse it!* (Number 23:19-20).

10

Jezebel Fast

"Then Jezebel wrote letters in Ahab's name, sealed them with his seal, and sent them to the elders and nobles who lived with Naboth in his city. In the letters, she wrote: "Proclaim a fast and give Naboth a seat of honor among the people. But seat two scoundrels opposite him and have them testify, 'You have cursed both God and the king!' Then take him out and stone him to death." (I Kings 21:8-10).

Many other religions in the world practice fasting, not just Christianity or Judaism. However, they are not fasting to the God of the universe but to their own deity. Some have good intentions for fasting, while some clearly do not. As was the case when Queen Jezebel called a fast. Although there is no indication that she actually fasted, she wrote letters to the elders and nobles in the town to call fast. However, this fast was not about seeking the heart of God. It was an evil plot to strike with the fist of wickedness (see Isaiah 58:4).

Fist of Wickedness

The purpose of fasting to strike with a fist of wickedness is usually to express anger, exact revenge, or kill innocent people. One example is when King Saul bound his men to an oath forbidding them to eat or drink until he avenges himself on his enemies (See 1 Samuel 14:24). This kind of fast is unacceptable to God because they do not seek the Lord's will. They have already made up in their minds what they want from their fast, and it has nothing to do with honoring God.

You can find another example of a wicked fast in Acts 23:14, when a group of men took an oath to fast until they killed the apostle Paul in Jerusalem. *"They came to the chief priests and elders and said, 'We have bound ourselves under a great oath that we will eat nothing until we have killed Paul."* They were trying to kill him because they did not like the resurrection message he preached. Their wicked scheme was thwarted, and Roman soldiers escorted Apostle Paul to safety. This was a common practice in Israel for people to take oaths and not eat in order to strike others with the *fist of wickedness.* So Jezebel's wicked fasting was not so far-fetched. Let's dig deep into this wicked fast to understand how God responds to such a terrible thing.

Naboth's Vineyard

It all began when King Ahab wanted to purchase Naboth's vineyard, "But Naboth replied, *"The Lord forbid I should give you the inheritance that was passed down by my ancestors."* (1 Kings 21:3). Naboth followed the law: *"The land must never be sold on a permanent basis, for the land belongs to Me. You are only foreigners and tenant farmers working for me."* (Leviticus 25:23 N). Furthermore, the law also states that. *"None of the territorial lands may pass from tribe to tribe, for all the land given to each tribe must remain within the tribe to which it was first allotted."* (Numbers 36:7 NLT). The king of Israel should have known this since this was the law of the land. Instead, King Ahab went home sad and angry and refused to eat. When his wife Jezebel inquired why he was so upset, he told her that it was because Naboth refused to sell him his vineyard. She cheered him up and told her she would get him the vineyard.

Jezebel's Wicked Scheme

Jezebel came up with this wicked scheme to get her husband the vineyard. She wrote letters in the king's name, called a fast, and got two people to accuse Naboth of blasphemy and have him killed. Why in the world would Jezebel call a fast for such an evil, wicked scheme? Apparently, fasting means different things to different people. The Jews viewed fasting as holy, but to Jezebel, it was just another public gathering that could be used for evil purposes.

She also needed two witnesses because they could not sentence a person to death upon the testimony of only one witness. Deuteronomy 19:15-19: *"You must convict no one of a crime on the testimony of only one witness. The facts of the case must be established by the testimony of two or three witnesses."* So Jezebel knew the laws of the Israelites, and she used them to her advantage when they suited her evil purposes.

During the fast, the two liars accused Naboth of cursing God and the king and stoned him to death. Although Jezebel didn't actually fast, she used the holy ordinance of fasting to lure Naboth out of his home, which ultimately caused his demise. She also uses God's law to condemn an innocent man to death. Although the wicked scheme worked, it was not unnoticed by God.

God's Response

Even in a wicked fast that was not done to honor God, He still sends His response. God sends the prophet to pronounce judgment on Ahab and his family for the wickedness that he and Jezebel had done to Naboth. 1 Kings 21:17-19 says, *"Then the word of the Lord came to Elijah the Tishbite: "Go down to meet Ahab, king of Israel, who rules in Samaria. He is now in Naboth's vineyard, where he has gone to take possession of it. Say to him, 'This is what the Lord says: Have you not murdered a man and seized his property?' Then say to him, 'This is what the Lord says: In the place where dogs licked up Naboth's blood, dogs will lick up your blood—yes, yours!"* God will not leave himself without a witness, so he will always send a prophetic warning before he sends judgment.

Ahab's Fast

With such a terrible prophetic word, it was time to seek God's heart. Ahab's response must have shocked everyone who knew him, because he bowed himself down to sackcloth and ashes, fasting before the Lord. *"But when Ahab heard this message, he tore his clothing, dressed in burlap, and fasted. He even slept in burlap and went about in deep mourning."* (1 Kings 21:27). After all the terrible things he and his wife was doing in Israel, how could Ahab hope to receive any grace from God?

Observe how Ahab fasted. He tore his clothes, dressed in burlap, and even slept in them. He was genuinely remorseful about what he had done. He was desperate to touch the heart of God. One almost feels sorry for Ahab. He was just a puppet on Jezebel's strings. He did whatever she wanted him to do. It was almost like he couldn't help himself. However, when he came face to face with his sins, through the prophetic word he received, he humbled himself before God and repented. God wants this kind of response when he sends a prophetic word.

The prophetic word is meant to lead us to repentance, and that's exactly what Ahab did. He knew that Elijah was no false prophet and that God would do exactly what Elijah said. He had seen the drought, the Mount Carmel massacre, and the rain after the drought. So the only thing he could do with such devastating prophetic utterance was to fast and pray.

God Relented

The Lord took note of Ahab's fasting and sent the Prophet Elijah to speak to him a second time. *"Then the word of the Lord came to Elijah the Tishbite: "Have you noticed how Ahab has humbled himself before me?*

Because he has humbled himself, I will not bring this disaster in his day, but I will bring it to his house in the days of his son." (1 Kings 21:28-29) Although Ahab conspired to commit murder, his fasting touched the heart of God because he believed in God's prophet, and he was genuinely sorrowful for what he had done. He repented and humbled himself, and God relented from sending judgment in Ahab's lifetime.

Although Ahab repented, there is no sign that Jezebel ever repented. God was willing to forgive even Jezebel, but she refused to repent. He said, *"I have given her time to repent of her immorality, but she is unwilling."* (Revelation 2:21). Jezebel lived many years after the death of Ahab but did not repent. Jezebel later received a severe punishment for her wickedness. Her judgment came when Jehu became king. He killed all of Ahab's family, including Jezebel. He ordered her Eunuchs, *"Throw her down!" So they threw her out the window, and her blood spattered against the wall and on the horses. And Jehu trampled her body under his horses' hooves."* (2 Kings 9:33).

So fasting to strike with the fist of wickedness will not yield pleasant results because Jezebel met a terrible death, just like the prophet predicted. *"When they went out to bury her, they found nothing but her skull, her feet, and the palms of her hands. So they went back and told Jehu, who replied, "This is the word of the LORD, which He spoke through His servant Elijah the Tishbite: 'On the plot of ground at Jezreel, the dogs will devour the flesh of Jezebel.* (2 Kings 9:35-36).

Although Ahab was killed in battle, he died a more honorable death than Jezebel because they buried him with his fathers as a king of Israel. The judgment was for both of them, for their wickedness. However, Ahab repented, but Jezebel did not, and they both met different fates.

The takeaway from Jezebel's fast is that people can fast for the wrong reason, but God, in His infinite mercy, will give them time to repent. He will always send a prophetic warning before he sends judgment because He prefers to show mercy. So although this fasting didn't begin with a prophetic word, it ended with one. Some fasting began because of a prophetic word, while others ended with a prophetic word. Always look for or listen to the prophetic word when you fast because it's the channel through which God answers your prayers.

Call to Action

When we stray from the path of righteousness, God will send a prophet to tell us of our sins. Keep in mind it is unnecessary for someone to hold the official title of a prophet to be used by God. God can use anyone or anything He pleases, even a donkey. He gives us the Holy Spirit to help us discern or recognize when He is speaking through another person, a video, a book, or a song to bring convictions to our hearts. Remember, the essence of prophecy is to testify of Jesus, and to testify of Jesus means we are testifying of His marvelous work of salvation. So when the Holy Spirit convicts us of our sins through a prophetic word, we must choose to repent and return to God.

If God sends you a prophetic warning, take a moment to assess your heart. Warnings are not meant to punish you; they are intended to correct your behavior and guide you to the path of righteousness. When the tornado siren sounds, it warns you to take shelter before the storm reaches you. Likewise, when God sends people to warn you, it is only a siren to alert you to impending disaster. When God reveals hidden sins in our hearts, there is only one thing to do: acknowledge them and repent. God will protect you from judgment if you obey His prophetic warnings and repent, as King Ahab did.

So as you fast today, ask the Holy Spirit to help you understand and discern your motive for fasting. Understanding your desires when you fast will make a huge impact on the outcome of your fast. Let your fasting desires be to touch the heart of God, and everything else you desire will fall into place. Never fast to cause harm to anyone because it will come back to haunt you. Fasting should be used as a tool of repentance, as with Ahab. The Lord really delights in showing mercy. As evil as Ahab was, his fasting touched the heart of God, and God gave him mercy.

Promise: *"Then the LORD will be zealous for His land and pity His people."* (Joel 2:18)

11

Samuel Fast

"Then Samuel said, "Assemble all Israel at Mizpah, and I will intercede with the Lord for you." When they had assembled at Mizpah, they drew water and poured it out before the Lord. On that day, they fasted, and there they confessed, "We have sinned against the Lord." Now Samuel was serving as leader of Israel at Mizpah." (1 Samuel 7:5-6)

The people of Israel were in great distress because of the oppression of the Philistines. The Ark of the Covenant was captured, and after spending five months in the Philistine camp, they miraculously returned it to Israel. It stayed at a place called Kirjath Jearim for 20 years. During this time, Israel was in deep mourning because they felt like God had abandoned them. Samuel, their priest, and judge at that time, called a solemn assembly, and all the people assembled at Mizpah, where he interceded to God on their behalf. This is one of the most interesting fast I encountered in the Bible. On the day of the fast, the people did seven interesting things.

The first thing they did was get rid of their idols. Samuel prophesied to them, *"If you want to return to the Lord with all your hearts, get rid of your foreign gods and your images of Ashtoreth. Turn your hearts to the*

Lord and obey him alone; then he will rescue you from the Philistines." So *the Israelites got rid of their images of Baal and Ashtoreth and worshiped only the Lord."* (1 Samuel 7:3-4). Getting rid of their idols meant they burnt or destroyed them. It also indicates their willingness to forsake their idols and return to God in repentance. They were willing to lay aside anything that would impede their relationship with God.

The second thing they did was assemble themselves before God. This was a Holy convocation in which the people consecrated themselves to God. Regular gatherings were held at specific times each year, but this was not one of them. This was like an emergency meeting. Usually, assemblies like these interrupt routine daily activities. There was a deep sense of hunger for God mixed with a desperate desire to be rescued from the Philistines. They were willing to do whatever it took to touch the heart of God, so they obeyed the prophetic instructions that Samuel gave them.

Drink Offering

The third act they performed was to pour water before the Lord. *"When they had assembled at Mizpah, they drew water and poured it out before the Lord. On that day, they fasted and confessed, "We have sinned against the Lord."* (1 Samuel 7:6). As I contemplated their actions, I wondered what was the significance of their water offerings to God. That was not part of the prophetic instructions, but God does not appear to reject it.

Pouring water on the ground is not one of God's prescribed offerings in the Tabernacle, although it could be considered a drink offering instead of wine or oil. In biblical times, a drink offering was a libation of wine, milk, or oil made with other sacrifices.

Before Moses's laws, we had no record of what was considered a drink offering, but it is conceivable that water was used as a drink offering. The earliest form of drink offering was recorded in Genesis

35:14 when Jacob set up a pillar of stone in the place where the Lord spoke with him, and he poured out a drink offering on it; he also poured oil on it. Observe that he *"also poured oil,"* so the oil was in addition to something else, such as wine or water; we do not know. So it is uncertain when the practice of pouring out water before the Lord began, but it could have been as early as in the wilderness days.

In fact, Moses was the first to pour water on the ground at the Lord's command, although it was for an entirely different reason. In Exodus 4:9, The Lord told Moses, *"But if they do not believe these two signs or listen to you, take some water from the Nile and pour it on the dry ground. The water you take from the river will become blood on the ground."* Therefore, water libation was not an entirely strange practice. They probably used it many times after this initial use but for different purposes. The most famous of water poured out before the Lord in the Bible is when Elijah poured water on the sacrifice in Mount Carmel. (I Kings 18:33). Even to this day, Jews continue to pour water before God as a drink offering.

Our lives are like Water.

Water is precious to the Israelites because they view water as the source of creation and the origination of all life forms, as a blessing and covenant, and as the source of cleansing and purification. So when they pour out the water before God, they were really offering it as a sacrifice to God. They had to draw the water from a well and physically carry it to a certain point to pour it out before God. This was a tremendous sacrifice, especially in a region where water is scarce. It's like going to the supermarket to purchase your week's supply of drinking water and then going into your backyard and pouring out all of it on the ground.

In the Samuel fast, however, the people were pouring this water out as an indication that they were pouring their lives out to God. 2

Samuel 14:14 says, *"Our lives are like water poured out on the ground, which cannot be gathered up again."* So when they poured out the water as an offering to the Lord, they were essentially saying to God we are pouring out our lives before you, and we will obey you, even if it costs us our lives. We see this exemplified by the Apostle Paul in Philippians 2:17. He said, *"But even if I am being poured out like a drink offering on the sacrifice and service coming from your faith, I am glad and rejoice with all of you."* This means that he was willing to pour out his life like water on the ground to serve God in whatever capacity God wanted him to. He had no concern for his personal well-being. His only focus was to please God in every way.

When King David was in exile and longed to drink water from a well in Bethlehem, his men broke through the Philistine battle lines, drew some water from the well by the gate in Bethlehem, and brought it back to him, *but he refused to drink it. Instead, he poured it out as an offering to the Lord. "The Lord forbid I should drink this!" he exclaimed. "This water is as precious as the blood of these men who risked their lives to bring it to me." So David did not drink it. Instead, he poured it out as an offering to the Lord."* (2 Samuel 23:16-17). To David, this water represents the lives of his men, and the only thing he could do with it was offered it to God as a drink offering.

Another reason they offered water to God was for repentance. Lamentations 2:19 says, *"Rise during the night and cry out. Pour out your hearts like water to the Lord. Lift up your hands to him in prayer, pleading for your children, for they are faint with hunger in every street."* So pouring out water to the Lord indicates they were pouring out their hearts in repentance to the Lord because they were sorry for their sins and wanted to repent.

Confession
The fourth thing they did was acknowledge and confess their sins.

This is essential in any fasting endeavor because God only accepts our fasting and sacrifices when we confess and repent of our sins. *"If we confess our sins, he is faithful and just and will forgive us our sins and purify us from all unrighteousness."* (1 John 1:9).

Sometimes we do not get the desired result when we pray because we do not confess and repent. And we do not confess our sins because we do not know what they are. Therefore, as you fast, ask the Lord to reveal your sins to you, then confess and repent from them.

The fifth thing the people did was fast all day before God. This fasting was a representation of the Day of Atonement. On the Day of Atonement, the people would assemble before the Lord and fast all day as the priest made atonement for their sins. Leviticus 23: 26-28 details for us the laws of the day of atonement. *"Then the LORD said to Moses, "Be careful to celebrate the Day of Atonement on the tenth day of that same month—nine days after the Festival of Trumpets. You must observe it as an official day for holy assembly, **a day to deny yourselves** and present special gifts to the LORD. Do no work during that entire day because it is the Day of Atonement, when offerings of purification are made for you, making you right with the LORD your God.* So the people sanctified themselves according to the laws of the Lord as Samuel made atonement for them.

Priestly Intercession

The sixth thing they did was ask the priest to make intercession for them. Although the people confessed their sins and repented, they asked the priest to pray for them. *"They said to Samuel, "Do not stop crying out to the Lord our God for us, that he may rescue us from the hand of the Philistines."* (1 Samuel 7:8). They understood the importance of a priestly prayer and the power of agreement.

It is important to be connected to a body of believers and to understand those who have authority over you. Their prayers may very well save your lives. Ecclesiastes 4:12 says *A person standing alone* can be attacked and defeated, but two can stand back-to-back and conquer. Three are even better, for a triple-braided cord is not easily broken. If your pastor is unavailable to pray with you, you can agree with a brother or sister in Christ because there is power in agreement.

The seventh thing they did was offer a young lamb to God as a burnt offering. Samuel understands that his priestly intercession is not complete without a sin offering. *"So Samuel took a young lamb and offered it to the Lord as a whole burnt offering. He pleaded with the Lord to help Israel, and the Lord answered him."* (1 Samuel 7:9). It is fitting for Samuel to offer a young lamb, as this young lamb without blemish represents the atoning work of Jesus Christ, the lamb of God, that takes away the sins of the world.

The people sinned against God by worshiping idols, so atonement was needed to cover their sins. Again, this was not part of the prophecy, but it was part of their act of faith in returning to God. They understood that returning to God meant they had to make the required sacrifice to atone for their sins. Sometimes there are necessary actions that we must take in order to accept Christ's atoning work. We may have to forgive someone or stop doing something we know is sinful. This represents our act of faith and our desire to obey God.

God's Answer

Samuel and the people had successfully touched the heart of God through sincere fasting and genuine repentance to God. So God answered their prayers, *"Just as Samuel was sacrificing the burnt offering, the Philistines arrived to attack Israel. But the Lord spoke with a mighty voice of thunder from heaven that day, and the Philistines were thrown into such confusion that the Israelites defeated them."* (1 Samuel 7:10). As long as Samuel remained their judge, the Philistines did not invade Israel again, and the people continued to obey the laws of the Lord. Notice that a prophetic word was given, and the people obeyed, and

God answered their prayers and rescued them from the Philistine, just as he promised if they repented. This shows us that God is faithful to do what he says if we obey his prophetic instructions.

Call to Action

Do you feel like God has abandoned you and your enemies have risen against you? Maybe you tried to get rid of some besetting sins in your life, but that didn't work, or you offered your life to God in service, but you are still far from where you believe God wants you to be. Maybe you even asked your pastor to pray with you or for you concerning these issues, but still no answer.

Many times we do not get answers to our prayers because we do not fast or pray correctly. Sometimes it's only when we face an enemy that is too powerful for us that we recognize how far we have wandered from God. If you feel like God has abandoned you, remember He never leaves us or forsakes, but we have a tendency to wander from him.

So as you fast and pray today, do what these Israelites did. They received a prophetic word and chose to believe and act on it. They got rid of their idols; they assembled before the Lord, poured water before the Lord, acknowledged and confessed their sins, fasted all day, asked the priest to pray, and offered a sacrifice. They repented and returned to God. You may say, but I do not have any idols; think about the things that take priority over prayer and opportunities to worship God. Those things are your idols.

Return to God wholeheartedly by laying aside everything that does not glorify Him. He said those that come to him he will not cast out, and if we confess our sins to him, he is faithful and just to forgive us of our sins. Let us accept the blood of Jesus, our unblemished lamb, as our sin offering, giving us peace with God and reconciling us with Him. It doesn't matter how badly you mess up; choose to return to him with your whole heart through fasting and prayer. He will forgive and reconcile you to Himself.

Promise: *The LORD will open the heavens, His abundant storehouse, to send rain on your land in season and to bless all the work of your hands. You will lend to many nations but borrow from none.* (Deuteronomy 28:12)

12

National Fast

This is the proclamation he issued in Nineveh: "By the decree of the king and his nobles: Do not let people or animals, herds or flocks taste anything; do not let them eat or drink. But let people and animals be covered with sackcloth. Let everyone call urgently on God. Let them give up their evil ways and their violence. Who knows? God may yet relent and with compassion turn from his fierce anger so that we will not perish." (Jonah 3:7-9).

God loves the nations of the world and desires to save them, but they rarely see their sins or their need for salvation. It usually takes calamity or danger to draw our attention back to God. Nineveh was an ungodly nation, but desired to show them mercy, so He sent the prophet Jonah to warn them of impending disaster. The entire nation heeded the warnings, repented, fasted, and prayed, and God answered their prayers. This is remarkable because many times, when prophetic messages are given to an entire nation, there are usually mixed responses. Some will mock and scoff at the prophecy, while others will heed the warning, but this entire nation turned to God in just three days, even their animals.

This Nineveh situation has caused me to think about what's happening in our nation. God has shown me several prophetic visions for America, leading me to believe that America shall be saved. There are several prophecies concerning America's future, some good and some not so good. Either way, each prophecy has mixed reactions because the entire nation has not turned to God. But there is still a possibility that God can cause this to happen in the future, but we continue to experience mixed reactions to God's prophetic warnings.

The Battering Ram

In 2020, I received a prophetic word concerning President Trump. It was a very puzzling word, so I kept it to myself, but only now that I saw some of its fulfillment on January 6th, 2021, that I feel at liberty to share it. Almost everything in the prophecy came through.

I had a vision of a battering ram battering down an ancient but sturdy-looking gate. There were people behind the gate, inside a complex that looked like a luxury hotel, but they didn't seem to know that war was at their gate. There were two huge gate pillars on either side of this huge ancient gate, and people were trying to get into the complex without going through the gate. The battering ram continued to attack the gate until it broke down, and the people rushed inside the complex. The people inside the complex were surprised and sprang to their feet and started defending themselves.

As I prayed about the vision, the Lord said; *President Trump is My battering ram for America. Much of what America trusts in will be shaken as he plows through America. Political, military, and economic power has become America's gods, and they must be shaken. They use My blessings as walls and fortresses of protection, which causes them to stop trusting Me. Therefore I have given them a President who will shatter the things they put above Me. However, I will leave its foundation in place because it is holy.*

Trump is my trumpet for America but also my instrument of judgment. The battering ram is not what people should fear but what comes after the gate is breached. The actual attack is the political, economic, and military breakdown. The real attack is the deadly war that is knocking on America's door.

I am long-suffering and kind, but I cannot save people who do not want to be saved. Most people do not see their need to be saved, hence the battering ram. But if America will heed their warning and return Me as their deliverer, I will come to them, restore their fortunes, and show them mercy, just as I did for Nineveh. I know there will be a mixed reaction to this prophecy; that is why it is so interesting and miraculous that the *whole* nation of Nineveh heard a simple prophetic word and repented. Let's explore the Nineveh fast to understand how it applies to us today.

Nineveh Fast

Nineveh was an evil city, but God wanted to save them, and the only way He could do that was to give them a chance to repent of their wickedness. So God sent the prophet Jonah to warn the people of Nineveh. *"Go to the great city of Nineveh and preach against it, because its wickedness has come up before me."* (Jonah 1:2). Initially, Jonah tried to run away from his assignment on a ship headed to Tarshish, but a great storm rose up on the sea, and the people on the ship cast lots to find out who caused the storm. The lot fell to Jonah, and he asked to be thrown overboard. A great fish swallowed him, and he prayed to God while in the fish's belly. After three days, *The Lord spoke to the fish, and it vomited Jonah onto dry land.* Jonah 2:10

God gave Jonah a second chance to proclaim His prophetic warning to the people of Nineveh. Now the word of the Lord came to Jonah the second time, saying, *"Arise, go to Nineveh, that great city, and preach to it the message that I tell you."* So Jonah arose and went to Nineveh, according to the word of the Lord. (Jonah 3:1-3).

God could have allowed Jonah to die in the belly of the whale, but He did not give up on Jonah; He gave him a second chance. Jonah's second chance was also Nineveh's second chance because they were able to hear the word of the Lord. Jonah's prophetic message was very simple, although it took him three days to go through the city and warn them.

Jonah's Message

His Prophetic message did not come with a lot of profound revelation and exhortation. Jonah went through the city of Nineveh and declared, *"Forty more days until Nineveh is overturned."* Jonah's only purpose was to warn the people that their nation was in danger of destruction. He had no control over how they responded. He didn't give them any instruction on how to avoid the pending destruction. All he did was warn them of what was coming, and the people responded to the warning.

Similarly, prophets today have no control over how people respond to their messages. Their only responsibility is to warn, but it is the hearer's responsibility to respond accordingly. In recent years, many genuine prophets have warned of pending destruction, but it is met with skepticism, indifference, doubts, and unbelief. Some people are heeding the prophetic warnings, while others are disregarding them.

Historically, many nations have been destroyed because they failed to heed God's prophetic messages. The Lord warned Israel several times that disaster was coming, but they did not heed His warnings, and disaster came. If God didn't withhold disaster from his chosen people when they refuse to repent, will he withhold it from us?

The Lord is still holding out his hands to us today, saying, *"If my people who are called by my name will humble themselves and pray and seek my face and turn from their wicked ways, I will hear from heaven and will forgive their sins and restore their land."* (2 Chronicles 7:14)

God is not interested in destruction as much as he is interested in showing mercy. He has no pleasure in the death of the wicked, and He rejoices over one sinner that repents. He will always send a prophetic warning before He sends destruction, but we must respond appropriately. That's the reason he sent the prophet Jonah to warn the people of Nineveh and is the same reason he is sending prophets to warn the nations today.

The People's Response

The people of Nineveh believed the prophet Jonah and proclaimed a desperate fast; from the greatest to the least of them put on sackcloth and humbled themselves before God. *"When Jonah's warning reached the king of Nineveh, he rose from his throne, took off his royal robes, covered himself with sackcloth, and sat down in the dust. This is the proclamation he issued in Nineveh: "By the decree of the king and his nobles: Do not let people or animals, herds or flocks taste anything; do not let them eat or drink. But let people and animals be covered with sackcloth. Let everyone call urgently on God. Let them give up their evil ways and their violence. Who knows? God may yet relent and with compassion turn from his fierce anger so that we will not perish."* (Jonah 3:5-9).

The entire nation fasted before the Lord, from the king to the cattle. Besides giving up food and drink, they also gave up their evil ways and cried out to God for mercy. Why did the people of Nineveh respond in such a way? God has issued similar prophetic warnings to other nations in the past, but they failed to respond as Nineveh did.

The king's willingness to fast and pray led the entire nation to do the same. A wise leader can make a huge difference in the success of a nation. For example, In 1863, during a time of war, President Abraham Lincoln recognized the need for national prayer and fasting and proclaimed a solemn assembly.

The proclamation read as follows; *"It is the duty of nations as well as of men to own their dependence upon the overruling power of God, to confess their sins and transgressions, in humble sorrow, yet with assured hope that genuine repentance will lead to mercy and pardon; and to recognize the sublime truth, announced in the Holy Scriptures and proven by all history, that those nations only are blessed whose God is the Lord.*

And, insomuch as we know that, by His divine law, **nations like individuals are subjected to punishments and chastisements** *in this world, may we not justly fear that the awful calamity of civil war, which now desolates the land, may be but a punishment, inflicted upon us, for our presumptuous sins, to the needful end of our national reformation People? We have been the recipients of the choicest bounties of heaven. We have been preserved, these many years, in peace and prosperity. We have grown in numbers, wealth, and power as no other nation has ever grown* **but we have forgotten God.**

We have forgotten the gracious hand that preserved us in peace and multiplied and enriched and strengthened us, and we have vainly imagined, in the deceitfulness of our hearts, that some superior wisdom and virtue of our own produced all these blessings. Intoxicated with unbroken success, we have become too self-sufficient to feel the necessity of redeeming and preserving grace, **too proud to pray to the God that made us!**

It behooves us then to humble ourselves before the offended Power, to confess our **national sins,** *and to pray for clemency and forgiveness."* ~ President Abraham Lincoln.

With this proclamation, President Lincoln designated a day of national humiliation, fasting, and prayer on Thursday, April 30th, 1863. Shortly after this, the North won two major battles at Gettysburg and Vicksburg, signaling the turning point of the civil war and the ultimate victory for the North.

Many other battles have been won throughout history because whole nations or armies choose to fast and pray. Another famous example is the Roman Emperor Constantine, who attributed his military victory over his enemies to his acknowledgment and prayers to the living God. No doubt, there are many other unknown victories that are won as a result of divine intervention. So fasting and prayer make a massive difference in the outcomes of pending national disasters.

God's Response

Recently the Lord told me that an atomic move of God is coming to the earth, but it will come through global fasting and prayer. As we look around today, many fasting and prayer movements are taking place, but it's a mixed multitude. Some people are genuinely seeking God, while others are fasting to seek help for their personal needs. Whatever the reason behind each fast, God knows exactly how to reach each person's heart. As we saw in the previous fast, God still sent His prophetic word even though the fast was not done with the correct motives. God knows how to correct and humble each person as they fast and pray to him.

The interesting thing about Nineveh's fast was not how Nineveh prayed but what they did that caused God to relent from sending the destruction he promised. They didn't really know how to pray, but their fasting actions became their prayer. Their only objective in fasting was to be spared from judgment. Somehow they understood that if they fasted, they would touch the heart of God, and that's exactly what happened. *"When God saw what they did and how they turned from their evil ways, he relented and did not bring on them the destruction he had threatened."* (Jonah 3:10). God had compassion for the people and spared the city of Nineveh because they responded in reverential fear of God.

Another reason God relented from sending disaster is that the people of Nineveh didn't know Him. They had no convictions of sin, and it would be unjust for God to send destruction without sending a warning. This is the reason God asked Jonah, *"Should I not have concern for the great city of Nineveh, in which there are more than a hundred and twenty thousand people who cannot tell their right hand from their left—and also many animals?"* Jonah 4:11. They couldn't discern the error of their ways, and if they did, they didn't know what to do about it until Jonah showed up. God wanted to show mercy to Nineveh; therefore, he sent his prophet to warn them that judgment was coming.

Call to Action

God is still interested in national fasting and repentance, especially considering what's happening in our nation and in the world today. Sin has never been more rampant than it is in our modern culture. It will take a move of God to alert us of the danger of this rapid moral decline and pull us up out of the great canyon of apostasy. However, this move will not happen without much fasting and prayer, but what will it take to cause people to really fast and pray as a nation? Genuine fasting and prayer do not happen until there is deep desperation in the hearts of man. Right now, the stage is set for mass desperation all around the world. Global plagues, sporadic and regional famines, political instability, economic downturns, and quite possibly World War III. All sorts of things are happening in our world that are beyond our control, and our only hope is found in our faith in God.

God is still sending prophets to warn, but it seems like no one is listening. People continue with their lives as if everything is OK while major rivers are drying up and droughts and famines, wars, economic collapse, and political upheaval are happening in various parts of the world.

People are not observing the signs of the time, but when they become desperate enough, they will cry out to God. The people of Nineveh were desperate for a move of God, and their desperation caused them to fast and pray fervently that God would relent from sending judgment.

God is giving us a second chance to repent of our sins, but it is up to us to heed His warnings. How we respond to the warning makes the difference in whether we receive judgment or mercy. If we want to touch the heart of God, as Nineveh did, we must fast, pray, and turn away from our sinful acts.

So as you fast and pray today, pray for national repentance for your nation. Pray that God will send true prophets to warn of any impending disasters. Pray that intercessors will arise and weep and pray over the nations. Remember, God says, ask me for the nations, and I will give them to you as an inheritance. Pray for the salvation of the nations. Pray for your families, communities, and churches to repent and turn to God. Pray for godly leaders who will respond like the king of Nineveh and President Abraham Lincoln, who will lead their nation to national repentance.

Promise: *No weapon formed against you shall prosper, and every tongue which rises against you in judgment You shall condemn.* (Isaiah 54:17).

13

Jehoshaphat Fast

Then some came and told Jehoshaphat, saying, "A great multitude is coming against you from beyond the sea, from Syria; and they are in Hazazon Tamar" (which is En Gedi). And Jehoshaphat feared and set himself to seek the Lord and proclaimed a fast throughout Judah. So, Judah gathered together to ask for help from the Lord; and from all the cities of Judah, they came to seek the Lord. (II Chronicles 20: 1-4).

We often lose battles we should have won because we do not engage the weapon of fasting and prayer. When Jehoshaphat heard that a vast army was coming against him, he became alarmed and bowed down to God in fasting and prayer.

Jehoshaphat's fast was not a routine or coerced fast; it was an automatic response to the distressing news he had heard. He knew that fasting and prayer was the quickest way to touch the Heart of God. We will analyze Jehoshaphat's fast, with a focus on how he approached God and responded to the prophetic instructions.

Proclaim a Fast

The first thing King Jehoshaphat did was proclaim a fast and bow down in humility before God. Although he was the king of Judah, he demonstrated humility by acknowledging his dependence on God. He prayed, *"O Lord God of our fathers, are You, not God in heaven and do You not rule over all the kingdoms of the nations, and in Your hand is there, not power and might so that no one is able to withstand You? Are You not our God, who drove out the inhabitants of this land before Your people Israel, and gave it to the descendants of Abraham, Your friend forever? (II Chronicles 20:6-7)*. Jehoshaphat acknowledged God has all power and can do anything.

Although he had not yet witnessed any great miracles during his lifetime, he knew about the miracles God performed for his forefathers. Jehoshaphat sincerely believed that God could deliver them because he knew God had done it before and could do it again. He believed God was still the same, yesterday, today, and forever. So he prayed by faith, believing God would answer him as He did for his ancestors. So Jehoshaphat continued praying, *"Your people settled here and built this temple to honor your name. They said, 'Whenever we are faced with any calamity such as war, plague, or famine, we can come to stand in your presence before this temple where your name is honored. We can cry out to you to save us, and you will hear us and rescue us.'* (II Chronicles 20:8-9).

Jehoshaphat was putting God in remembrance of His promise to King Solomon when he dedicated the temple. If they stood before the temple and cried out to God, He would hear and rescue them. Jehoshaphat also told The Lord that they were powerless against the great army that was coming against them, and they didn't know what to do, but their eyes were on Him.

The Prophet

As the king and the people continued seeking the face of God, a prophet told them, *"The Lord said, 'Do not be afraid or discouraged because of this vast army. For the battle is not yours, but God's. Tomorrow march down against them. They will climb up by the Pass of Ziz, and you will find them at the end of the gorge in the Desert of Jeruel. You will not have to fight this battle. Take up your positions; stand firm and see the deliverance the Lord will give you, Judah and Jerusalem. Do not be afraid; do not be discouraged. Go out to face them tomorrow, and the Lord will be with you."* (II Chronicles 20: 15-17).

The first thing God addressed was fear. He said, do not be afraid or be discouraged. Even when something massive is coming against us, we should not be afraid but only trust the Lord because the battle belongs to Him.

One question people frequently ask is, how do I know when to fight and when the battle belongs to the Lord? One way to know that the battle belongs to the Lord is when the battle is too much for you. God will never put more on you than you can bear. If the situation is beyond your control, then the battle belongs to God.

There was a time when I was experiencing some intense spiritual warfare, with demonic spirits attacking me in my sleep. Each night, I would get up and pray throughout the house, and it would leave. One night when the demonic spirit came to attack me, I looked at it and said, "It's you again? I am going to sleep." I rolled over and went back to sleep and slept like a baby. When I woke up the next morning, I had the feeling like my head was lying on Jesus's lap as I slept. Then I heard my spirit say, "Good Morning, Jesus. It's so good to wake up in your presence." I knew those words didn't come from my mind. I took note of the words and sort of pondered on them throughout the day. Later that afternoon, The Holy Spirit softly asked me, "Do you know why I came last night?" I replied, "No, Lord." He responded, "I came because the battle was too much for you." I was in awe! Now the words, *"heaven comes to fight for me,"* took on a whole new meaning.

This gives me great confidence in God and extinguishes any remaining doubts or fears, and that demonic thing never returned. You will fear nothing when you know The Lord is with you and fighting for you.

Set an Ambush

Jehoshaphat was in a situation where he needed to hear from the Lord quickly, so he fasted and received prophetic instructions from the Lord. This is another great example of how fasting births the prophetic. The prophet told him that he would not have to fight in the battle because the battle belonged to God. The prophetic word gave Jehoshaphat great confidence in The Lord, so he and his tiny army went out to face the massive army that came against them.

When Jehoshaphat sensed doubt among the people, he stopped and encouraged them, saying, *"Believe in the Lord your God, and you shall be established; believe His prophets, and you shall prosper."* (II Chronicles 20:20). He wanted the people to believe the prophetic word from The Lord and to trust God for victory.

Jehoshaphat embraced the prophetic word; he appointed singers and worshipers as they marched out to meet the vast army. Just like the prophet said, the people of God did not need to fight in that battle because God fought for them as they sang praises to Him. When the people sang praises to The Lord, He set ambushes and defeated the opposing army.

Never underestimate the power of your praise. It will set an ambush for your enemy. Your praise is truly a weapon that will bring your breakthrough. Keep praising God until you see the breakthrough, and don't forget to collect the plunder.

Collect the Plunder

Throughout our lives, we have all encountered situations beyond our control. God sometimes allows those situations to expose what is in our hearts and to plunder our enemies. God exposed the fear in

Jehoshaphat and the people, and when they chose to trust God; He gave them the opportunity to collect the plunder.

There was so much plunder that Jehoshaphat and his tiny army spent three days gathering valuables from the battlefield. Sometimes the great tragedy or trauma you defeat is directly proportional to the plunder that God wants to give you. *"When Jehoshaphat and his people came to take away their spoil, they found among them an abundance of valuables on the dead bodies, and precious jewelry, which they stripped off for themselves, more than they could carry away; and they were three days gathering the spoil because there was so much."* (II Chronicles 20:25).

God not only fights our battles for us when we fast, but He also permits us to take the plunder from the enemy. Has God ever done something so marvelous in your life that your haters just decided to leave you alone? God will give you rest on every side, too. If you fast and pray to Him, he will deliver you from all your fears. Not only did God fight their battles for them, but*"Because the fear of God was on all the kingdoms of those countries when they heard that the Lord had fought against the enemies of Israel. Then the realm of Jehoshaphat was quiet, for his God gave him rest all around.* (II Chronicles 20:29-30). So God gave them rest on every side.

Many times we fight battles and win the wars, but we do not collect the plunder. Sometimes we may have overcome a personal tragedy or trauma, but we never collect the plunder. Collecting the plunder could mean that you need to persevere and write a book, teach a course, start a nonprofit, or become an activist for a cause, etc. Collecting the plunder means using your freedom to free others. Jehoshaphat's men collected all the valuables from the dead bodies and were not ashamed to do so. Don't allow shame or pride to stop you from collecting the plunder. Tell your story because we are overcome by the blood of The Lamb and the word of our testimony. Testify today of what good things the Lord has done for you.

Sometimes your plunder will be your children, your health, and your finances. So do not leave the plunder on the battlefield. Yes, I know it is hard work to collect the plunder, but would you rather someone else collect your blessings? Be intentional about collecting the blessings that your battle has brought you.

Call to Action

Take a moment to think about what you're going through right now. Did you receive any prophetic words from The Lord? Are there any scriptures that apply to your situation? Are you praising God through your circumstances?

We do not always praise God when we receive a prophetic word because we wait to see its manifestation. Jehoshaphat and his tiny army didn't wait for the victory to start praising God. They praised God despite the powerful army camped against them because they had a prophetic word and believed it.

Sometimes we become weary because we are fighting battles on every side, financial, health, family, and national issues. When we face these challenges, we should do what Jehoshaphat did; we should humble ourselves in fasting and prayer, believe the prophetic word, believe that God will do what He says, praise the Lord and watch for His deliverance, then collect the plunder—and rest in the goodness of God. If we follow Jehoshaphat's example when facing battles too difficult for us to fight on our own, God will give us rest on every side.

So, as you fast today, think about what God says about your situation. When you pray, recognize that God has all power; believe He hears and answers your prayers. If you need healing, deliverance, or financial help, find relevant scriptures, pray them back to God, and sing praise to Him.

Sometimes, God will answer your prayer through a prophet, so pay attention to any prophetic utterances you receive concerning your situation. You might be one prophetic word away from your deliverance.

PROMISE: *"You will not need to fight in this battle. Position yourselves, stand still and see the salvation of the Lord, who is with you, do not fear or be dismayed.* (II Chronicles 20:17).

14

Hezekiah Fast

"When King Hezekiah heard this, he tore his clothes and put on sackcloth and went into the temple of the Lord. He sent Eliakim, the palace administrator, Shebna, the secretary, and the leading priests, all wearing sackcloth, to the prophet Isaiah, son of Amoz." (2 Kings 19:1-2).

Sometimes we face intimidating circumstances that are beyond our natural abilities to overcome. Maybe it is a debilitating sickness, a family crisis, or even a national crisis. Although things may look dismal and seem like there is no way out, that's not a time for us to throw our hands up in despair or sink into depression. That is the best time to fast, pray, and seek the face of God because the Lord is always close to the brokenhearted and those who are crushed in spirit.

King Hezekiah was facing a quandary when he heard that this great Assyrian army was coming against him. He didn't have the military power to face such a great, undefeated army. In fact, when the King Sennacherib of Assyria came out against him, Hezekiah offered a peace offering to the king rather than engage in a military battle. Hezekiah took all the silver and gold in his treasury and in the treasury of the Lord's temple, even the gold from the doorframe of the temple, and gave it to this evil king in an effort to appease him. His hope in doing so was that the king would withdraw his armed forces from the borders of Israel.

Let's go find out how Hezekiah successfully touched the heart of God and defeated this evil horde. In analyzing this fast, I hope you will learn strategies to help you defeat every intimidating circumstance you may encounter.

Defying the Lord of Host

The evil Assyrian king accepted the peace offering but did not withdraw his troops. Instead, he kept on intimidating and threatening to attack Israel. At one point, the commander of the Assyrian army blasphemed against the living God by telling the people, *"Don't let Hezekiah deceive you. He will never be able to rescue you from my power.* ***Don't let him fool you into trusting in the Lord*** *by saying, 'The Lord will surely rescue us. This city will never fall into the hands of the Assyrian king!'"* (2 Kings 18:29-30). This was an intimidation tactic to cause the people to doubt, but in his speech, not only the Assyrian commander defied King Hezekiah, but he also defied the Living God. His next statement was, *"What god of any nation has ever saved its people from my power? So what makes you think the Lord can rescue Jerusalem from me?"* (2 Kings 18:35). It's one thing for a person to disagree with you and even insult or attack you. Still, it's a whole different level when they speak against the Lord God Almighty.

More with us

The people did not respond to the intimidation tactics because Hezekiah encouraged the people to *"Be strong and courageous;* ***do not be afraid*** *nor dismayed before the king of Assyria, nor before all the multitude that is with him; for there are more with us than with him.* ***With him is an arm of flesh;*** *but* ***the Lord, our God, is with us,*** *to help us and to fight our battles."* And the people were strengthened by the words of Hezekiah, *king of Judah."* (2 Chronicles 32: 7-8). Fear is one of the first emotions we feel when facing an intimidating situation, so that's the first thing Hezekiah addressed in his people. He told them not to be afraid. Then he told them why they should not be afraid because it's not enough to tell people not to be afraid you should give them a place to put their concerns. They had genuine concerns because the army that came against them was undefeated. They had a track record of ravaging all the surrounding nations, and now they set their sights on Israel to do the same thing to them.

We should never underestimate the enemy's power, 'little p,' while we keep in mind the Power of our almighty God. Many people lose battles they should have won because they underestimate the power of their enemy. Sickness and disease can ravage and debilitate our lives. We must recognize the forces of darkness operating against our lives but rise above their power through faith in the Lord God almighty. The God that we serve is well able to deliver us. Even when we fall short, he is still willing to rescue us.

Hezekiah was confident that the Lord would deliver them, so he told the people the Assyrian army, though large in number, was only an army of flesh. The king of Assyria trusted in his many chariots and horsemen because he didn't know that the arm of flesh would always fail against the mighty living God. Hezekiah, like his forefather King David, knew not to trust in horses and chariots. He knew he could trust in the God of angel armies.

Hezekiah also used the words of the prophet Elisha to encourage the people. When a great army came out against Elisha, he told his servant the same thing Hezekiah told the people, *"Do not fear, for **those who are with us are more than those who are with them.**" And Elisha prayed, "Lord, I pray, open his eyes that he may see." Then the Lord opened the eyes of the young man, and he saw. And behold, the mountain was full of **horses and chariots of fire** all around Elisha."* (2 Kings 6:16-17).

The people were greatly encouraged and remained confident that God would somehow deliver them from this enemy horde.

Hezekiah sought the Lord

The next thing Hezekiah did was pray, fast, and seek the face of God while this ungodly army continued to threaten and intimidate them. King Hezekiah sought the Lord for His divine protection because he could see no natural way out. He had done everything he was capable of to prevent this war, and nothing was working. Hezekiah understood that his deliverance was not in his tiny army. His trust and confidence was in the Lord of the host to defeat this enemy horde and bring him victory.

He knew he could only trust in the Lord, his God, so he turned to the Lord in prayer. *"And so it was, when King Hezekiah heard it, that he tore his clothes, covered himself with sackcloth, and went into the house of the Lord. Then he sent Eliakim, who was over the household, Shebna the scribe, and the elders of the priests, covered with sackcloth, to Isaiah the prophet, the son of Amoz. And they said to him, "Thus says Hezekiah: '**This day is a day of trouble,** and **rebuke,** and **blasphemy**; for the children have come to birth, but there is **no strength to bring them forth**. It may be that the Lord your God will hear all the words of the Rabshakeh, whom his master, the king of Assyria, has sent to **reproach the living God,** and will rebuke the words which the Lord your God has heard. Therefore, lift up your prayer for the remnant that is left."* (2 Kings 19:1-4). When Hezekiah heard these blasphemous words against the living God, he went to the temple of the Lord to pray. Interestingly, he didn't seek help from his allies or give orders only to his advisors to fast and pray. He set the example by bowing himself down before God in sackcloth.

This was humility being modeled for the people, which is a key element in touching the heart of God when we pray. Hezekiah wanted them to know that although he was their king, he depended on the

Living God. He also wanted them to trust in the Lord for their deliverance, as he did. Not only did he enter the temple to pray, but he also sent his advisors to seek out the prophet Isaiah.

The Lords Response

So, as King Hezekiah fasted and prayed in the temple, the Lord sent His prophetic response. He sent his word through the prophet Isaiah. *"Say to your master, 'This is what the Lord says: Do not be disturbed by this blasphemous speech against Me from the Assyrian king's messengers. Listen! I myself will move against him, and the king will receive a message that he is needed at home. So he will return to his land, where I will have him killed with a sword."* (2 Kings 19:6-7). Hezekiah was encouraged by the prophetic message he received from Isaiah, but the enemy kept on taunting him.

Have you ever received a prophetic word of what the Lord is going to do in your life, but it seems like things only get worse? One mistake many people make when they receive a prophetic word is they discard it prematurely because it didn't happen when they expected it to happen. In this case, the prophetic word was given, but the enemy was still at their gates, intimidating them.

The King of Assyria sent a threatening letter to Hezekiah; *"This message is for King Hezekiah of Judah.* **Don't let your God, whom you trust, deceive you** *with promises the king of Assyria will not capture that Jerusalem. You know perfectly well what the kings of Assyria have done wherever they have gone. They have completely destroyed everyone who stood in their way! Why should you be any different?"* (2 Kings 19:10-11). So Hezekiah went back to the temple to pray. This time, he took the Sennacherib's blasphemous letter to the temple, spread it out before the Lord, and prayed, *"O Lord, God of Israel, you are **enthroned between the mighty cherubim!** You alone are God of all the kingdoms of the earth. **You alone created the heavens and the earth. Bend down, O Lord,** and listen! Open your eyes, O Lord, and see! Listen to Sennacherib's words of* defiance against the living God. *"It is true, Lord, that the kings of Assyria have destroyed all these nations. And they have thrown the gods of these nations into the fire and burned them. But, of course, the Assyrians could destroy them!* **They were not gods at all—only idols of wood and stone shaped by human hands.** *Now, O* **Lord our God, rescue us from his power;** *then all the kingdoms of the earth will know that you alone, O Lord, are God."* (2 Kings 19: 15-19). Pay close attention to how the king prayed because knowing how to pray is another key element to answered prayer. We don't always know how to approach God in prayer, and we say a bunch of empty words but nothing that God can really answer. In one of his many conversations with the Lord, the Prophet Bob Jones said the Lord told him to pray prayers that He could answer.

So the first thing that King Hezekiah did was acknowledge God as the Sovereign, mighty God who created the heaven and earth, and He rules over all the kingdoms of the earth.

My fear vanishes when I think about this great, big, majestic, all-powerful, glorious living God. And knowing that He fights for me even when I can't see Him releases tremendous peace and comfort in my soul.

The next thing the king did was acknowledge the power of his enemy; he reminded the Lord that the Assyrians defeated nations whose gods were only idols. In other words, this enemy threat was no idle threat, but the king believed that the mighty God of Israel could defeat this great army and give them victory. He knew no one could be against him if God was for him. No man, army, or even the Devil can defeat a person whose God is the one true and living God.

Angelic Intervention

So after Hezekiah fasted and prayed before the Lord, the word of the Lord came to the prophet Isaiah again. *"And this is what the Lord says* *about the king of Assyria: "His armies **will not enter Jerusalem**. They will not even shoot an arrow at it. They will not march outside its gates with their shields nor build banks of earth against its walls. The king will return to his own country by the same road on which he came. He will not enter this city, says the Lord. For **my own honor** and for the sake of my servant David, I will defend this city and protect it."* (2 Kings 19:32-34). The thing to understand here is that this was not a one-and-done battle. It took a while for Hezekiah to receive the manifestation of the prophetic word.

Although Hezekiah received the prophetic word of the Lord, he kept on praying. This is what old folks referred to as travailing prayers. He fully believed God's prophetic word would not return to him void. And this is another key element to answered prayers; you must believe that all things are possible with God.

Israel sinned against God, and they deserved punishment, but God was looking for a man or woman that would stand in the gap and travail for the nation, and Hezekiah was that man. So if you are praying about something that seems like it's not moving and the enemy is just stone-walling you. Just keep praying; that battle is not yours; it's the Lord.

Hezekiah was confident that the Lord heard his prayer because the prophet Isaiah sent this message to Hezekiah: *"This is what the Lord, the God of Israel, says: I have heard your prayer about King Sennacherib of Assyria."* (2 Kings 19:20). You can have this confidence in prayer, too, and just because a prophet did not come to you and specifically say to you, God has heard your prayers doesn't mean that He has not heard them. You have better than a prophet living inside you. You have The Holy Spirit in you, and He hears every prayer that you pray.

So the proof that God heard and answered Hezekiah's prayers came when *"the **angel of the Lord** went out to the Assyrian camp and killed 185,000 Assyrian soldiers. When the surviving Assyrians woke up the next morning, they found corpses everywhere. Then King Sennacherib of Assyria broke camp and returned to his own land. He went home to his capital of*

Nineveh and stayed there." (2 Kings 19:35-36). It doesn't take an entire angel army to defeat the armies of men; one angel can wipe out an entire battalion of soldiers.

Call to Action

When the hordes of hell are standing at your gate, you definitely want to hear from the Lord. I know you are not fasting out of doubt and unbelief but because you expect to hear from God. You expect Him to do something about the enemy that is standing at your gate.

Understanding how dependent we are on the Lord, God will drive us to fervently seek His face, which is what Hezekiah did. Seeking the Lord means that you have come to the end of yourself. You have exhausted your physical strength and resources. You know you don't have the strength or military might to fight against what is fighting against you, but you know that God's power is unlimited and that he will fight for you.

Hezekiah encouraged his people to trust the Lord of Host because the God of angel armies would fight for them. Sometimes when we face terrible circumstances and situations, we must be reminded that the God of angel armies is always by our sides. He is the one that fights our battles for us, and just because we can't always see in the spirit and see the angel armies, it doesn't mean that they are not there.

What are the intimidating issues that you are facing today? Does it feel like the enemy's knee is on your neck? You may even try to bargain with the devil for him to leave you alone, but nothing is working. That means it's time to humble yourself before the Lord, fast, pray, and believe in his mighty power to deliver you from all your fears. That is how I fight my battles with fasting and prayer.

So, as you fast and pray today, have faith in God and be confident that He has heard your prayers. After you pray, rest and wait for the manifestation of what you prayed for. The angel of the Lord is fighting for you, so you don't need to fight in this battle. Wait on the Lord and be of good courage, and he will give you victory even as you sleep. The Lord will always respond when we seek Him with all our hearts in fasting and prayer.

Promise: *"The Lord will fight for you; you need only to be still."* (Exodus 14:14)

15

Josiah Fast

"When the king heard what was written in the Book of the Law, he tore his clothes in despair." (2 Kings 22:11)

This fast is neatly tucked away in the chronicles of the kings of Israel that it has been relatively unnoticed. Yet it is one of the most remarkable yet simple fasts that touched the heart of God. It was conducted by one of Israel's youngest kings during a time when idol worship was at its peak.

More than worshiping idols, the people desecrated Solomon's temple and built altars and shrines for idol worship inside the temple. They also offered their children to be burned on altars as sacrifices to the idol Molech. So after three generations of ungodly kings, Josiah became king at eight years old.

And after reigning for eighteen years, he wanted to restore the temple of the Lord, so he hired workers to restore it. While the restoration process was underway, the priest of the Lord found the scrolls containing the laws of God. *"Hilkiah, the high priest said to Shaphan, the court secretary, "I have found the Book of the Law in the Lord's Temple!" Then Hilkiah gave the scroll to Shaphan, and he read it."*

(II Kings 22:8). Shaphan later read the scroll to King Josiah.

The Scroll

When King Josiah heard what was written in the scrolls, he broke down and wept before the Lord. *"Shaphan also told the king, 'Hilkiah, the priest has given me a scroll.' So Shaphan read it to the king. When the king heard what was written in the Book of the Law, he tore his clothes in despair."* (2 Kings 22:10-11). This was no ordinary weeping because the king recognized they were in deep trouble. Severe judgment was lapping at their gates, and they had done nothing to prevent what the Lord said would happen if they broke his laws.

King Josiah immediately sent his trusted servants to inquire of the Lord. *"Go, inquire of the Lord for me, for the people and for all Judah, concerning the words of this book that have been found; for great is the wrath of the Lord that is aroused against us, because our fathers have not obeyed the words of this book, to do according to all that is written concerning us."* (II Kings 22:13). Josiah's response was one of humility and godly sorrow.

This is a great example of how God wants us to respond when we sin against Him. Remember, Josiah was not the one who did the evil things that kindled the wrath of God; it was his forefathers, but he was the one now bearing the torch as the king of Israel. So it was up to him to do something about the mess that his forefathers left him. This is a prime example of why we should be careful what we sow since our children will inevitably reap the consequences. Often, children battle with the consequences of curses brought down to them by the sins of their fore parents. As Josiah realized the extent of the burden he was carrying because of the sins of his forefathers, he set his heart to seek God through His prophet. He wanted to find out how to correct the problem. He saw his ancestors had desecrated the temple and corrupted the nation by disobeying God, and he wanted to know how to fix it. So he inquired of the Lord through his advisors, who inquired of the prophet Huldah.

The Prophet

In those days, when people inquired of the Lord, they would go to the prophets. The prophet's job was to hear from the Lord and declare the Lord's words to the people. *"So Hilkiah the priest, Ahikam, Acbor, Shaphan, and Asaiah went to the New Quarter of Jerusalem to consult with the prophet Huldah. She was the wife of Shallum, son of Tikvah, son of Harhas, the keeper of the Temple wardrobe."* (2 Kings 22:14). As much as women get a bad rap for prophesying and teaching the word of God. I must pause here and tell you that five men in all went to one woman to hear the word of the Lord. They didn't care that she was a female. All they cared about was hearing from the Lord. But the question is, what was it about this woman that caused the king's men to seek her out? First, she was anointed to be a prophet, and secondly, she must have spent her days seeking the Lord and declaring His truths; how else would they have known that she was a prophet of the Living God?

God's Response

God always responds to those who genuinely seek Him, and Josiah was genuinely in his pursuit of God. I can imagine the Huldah was minding her own business when five of the king's men showed up at her door to inquire about the Lord. It must have frightened her because you must remember the spiritual conditions of the times she was living in. There were no true prophets in Israel, at least not in public. They had to go in hiding as the Baal and Asherah were being worshiped. Hilkiah, the priest, knew Huldah was a true prophet of God. Most like, he was familiar with her, and he must have told the others the best person to go to is Huldah; I know that she really hears from the Lord.

Listen, the Devil may have his henchmen, but God has his remnants. So the king's men went to Huldah because they knew she was a true prophet of God who could tell them what God said. *"She said to them, 'The Lord, the God of Israel, has spoken! Go back and tell the man who sent you, 'This is what the Lord says: I am going to bring disaster on this city and its people. All the words written in the scroll that the king of Judah has read will come true. For my people have abandoned me and offered sacrifices to pagan gods, and I am very angry with them for everything they have done. My anger will burn against this place and not be quenched.' "But go to the king of Judah who sent you to seek the Lord and tell him: 'This is what the Lord, the God of Israel, says concerning the message you have just heard:* **You were sorry and humbled yourself before the Lord** *when you heard what I said against this city and its people—that this land would be cursed and become desolate.* **You tore your clothing in despair and wept before me in repentance.** *And I have indeed heard you, says the Lord.* **So I will not send the promised disaster until after you have died** *and been buried in peace. You will not see the disaster I am going to bring on this city.'" So they took her message back to the king."* (2 Kings 22:15-20).

Observe what causes God to refrain from sending judgment in Josiah's time. Josiah was sorry and humbled himself, tore his clothes, and wept before the Lord; his fasting delayed judgment. He was repentant and showed godly sorrow over the sins of his ancestors.

Huldah's prophecy was more than remarkable because it happened just as she predicted. But even more interesting than that was Josiah's response to the prophecy. Josiah took her words to heart and initiated a tremendous reform throughout Israel.

Josiah Reform

The Josiah reformation is one of the most discussed topics of that time. According to the Bible, no other king completely followed the laws of Moses like Josiah did. It was like an unseen force was driving him to purge the nation. He even burned the bones of dead people to purge the land. *"The king summoned all the elders of Judah and Jerusalem. And the king went up to the Temple of the Lord with all the people of Judah and Jerusalem, along with the priests and the prophets—all the people from the least to the greatest. There, the king read to them the **entire Book** of the Covenant that had been found in the Lord's Temple. The king took his place of authority beside the pillar and renewed the covenant in the Lord's presence. **He pledged to obey the Lord by keeping all his commands, laws, and decrees with all his heart and soul.** In this way, he confirmed all the terms of the covenant that were written in the scroll, **and all the people pledged themselves to the covenant.***

Then the king instructed Hilkiah, the high priest and the priests of the second rank, and the Temple gatekeepers to remove from the Lord's Temple all the articles that were used to worship Baal, Asherah, and all the powers of the heavens. The king had all these things burned outside Jerusalem on the terraces of the Kidron Valley, and he carried the ashes away to Bethel. He did away with the idolatrous priests, who had been appointed by the previous kings of Judah, for they had offered sacrifices at the pagan shrines throughout Judah and even in the vicinity of Jerusalem. They had also offered sacrifices to Baal, the sun, the moon, the constellations, and all the powers of the heavens." (2 Kings 23:1-5)

This was equivalent to calling a solemn assembly. No fasting was noted, but most elders would have known that when an assembly like this was called, it was time to fast because the Lord was among them, exhorting them to get rid of their idols and return to him with fast and weeping.

Josiah continued the reformation throughout the land. After cutting down Asherah poles, destroying Baal altars, and killing their priest, he called the people back to real worship with the Living God. After all that house cleaning, it was time to celebrate. *"King Josiah then issued this order to all the people: "You must celebrate the Passover to the Lord your God, as required in this Book of the Covenant." There had not been a Passover celebration like that since the time when the judges ruled in Israel nor throughout all the years of the kings of Israel and Judah."* (2 Kings 23:21-22). So the people returned to God and celebrated the Passover in Israel for the first time in many years.

Call to Action

Many of you are dealing with circumstances brought on by generational curses that were not dealt with by your fore-parents. It's not enough to understand that the circumstances that you are facing are caused by generational curses. It's up to you to break those curses and do what is right in the eyes of the Lord. It is important to note that Josiah didn't commit the terrible acts of idolatry that were plaguing his nation, but he chose to do something about it and clean it up. You have a choice to make as you navigate your way through life. You can choose to follow in the footsteps of your forefathers, or you can choose to follow the laws of God. There comes a day of reckoning in everyone's life when they all must make this choice.

So as you fast and pray today, consider what generational curse you are dealing with personally. Consider what generational curse we are facing in our nation because of the ungodly things that were done in our nation. Many things will come to mind, both personally and nationally.

On the personal side, many people deal with the generational curse of depression, suicide, witchcraft, sexual abuse, teenage pregnancy, abortions, alcoholism, and a host of other issues.

On the national side, we are facing unresolved crimes committed by people with political powers, such as slavery, abortion, unjust laws, unfair justice systems, and a slew of other ungodly crimes. So our sins, just like Israel's sins, have reached up to the high heavens. Ask yourself what you can do to rectify these situations.

We need to become like King Josiah, humble ourselves in prayer, and seek forgiveness for ourselves and our nation. We may not go around and cut down shrines and statues, but we can certainly fast and pray with confidence, knowing that God hears and answer prayers in miraculous ways.

Promise: *"For I am about to do something new. See, I have already begun! Do you not see it? I will make a pathway through the wilderness. I will create rivers in the dry wasteland."* (Isaiah 43:19)

16

Jeremiah Fast

"In the ninth month of the fifth year of Jehoiakim, son of Josiah, king of Judah, a time of fasting before the Lord was proclaimed for all the people in Jerusalem and those who had come from the towns of Judah." (Jeremiah 36:9)

Sometimes we proclaim a fast, but we do not know why. We may fast because we see other people do it or we think that's what God wants us to do. If we fast in this manner, there is no guarantee of an answer from God, or He may give you an answer that you do not expect.

Although I called this chapter Jeremiah fast, it was King Jehoiakim who called a fast for all the people of Judah, but God sent the answer through the prophet Jeremiah. The people of Israel were under severe oppression from the Babylonians, who threatened to war against them. The king consecrated a fast as he had seen his predecessors do when faced with severe military threats.

In the previous chapter, we learned King Jehoshaphat proclaimed a fast when a great army came against Israel. He and all the people gathered before the Lord's temple to fast and seek the help of God. A prophet gave King Jehoshaphat a word from the Lord. The king accepted the prophetic word and acted according to the prophet's instructions.

As in the previous case, King Jehoiakim decrees a fast and gathers the people of Israel before the Lord. Similarly, the prophet Jeremiah received a message from the Lord and relayed it to King Jehoiakim. But his response and the result of his fasting were completely opposite to King Jehoshaphat's.

As we study this fast, our goal is to understand why the outcomes of this fast differed from previous fasts done in the same manner. Could it be that we are fasting, as Jehoiakim did? It is important to know how to tell if God has answered our prayers, especially if the answer He gives is not what we expect.

Fasting Day

On the day of the fast, God told Jeremiah, *"Get a scroll and write down all my messages against Israel, Judah, and the other nations. Begin with the first message back in the days of Josiah, and write down every message right up to the present time. Perhaps the people of Judah will repent when they hear* all the terrible things I have planned for them again. *Then I will be able to forgive their sins and wrongdoings."* (Jeremiah 36:2-3). In His goodness, God sent the prophet to warn them of the terrible things to come, hoping they would repent and return to Him. God offered his people the olive branch of repentance because he loved them and wanted them to be forgiven.

Jeremiah told Baruch, his scribe, I am restricted from going to the temple, *"So you go to the Temple on the next day of fasting and read the messages from the Lord that I have had you write on this scroll. Read them so the people who are there from all over Judah will hear them."* (Jeremiah 36:6). Baruch did as Jeremiah requested, and they relayed the message to the king on the day of the fast. This was to indicate to King Jehoiakim's fast that God was responding to his fasting.

Although we do not know what he prayed for, we know the answer he received was not what he wanted. Maybe he prayed for God to spare Israel from the Babylonians, and maybe he expected God to rescue them as He did in the past. Based on his response to the prophetic instructions he received from Jeremiah, we know that was certainly not what he expected. Let's review the king's response to determine what he expected from fasting.

Kings Response

When the king's scribes heard the message, *they looked at one another in alarm. "We must tell the king what we have heard," they said to Baruch."* (Jeremiah 36:16). They knew the king would not like the message, so they told Baruch and Jeremiah to hide while they relayed the message to the king.

The King was outraged because Jeremiah prophesied that the king of Babylon was going to destroy Israel. He cut up the scroll and threw it into the fire. *"Each time Jehudi finished reading three or four columns, the king took a knife and cut off that section of the scroll. He then threw it into the fire, section by section, until the whole scroll was burned up. Neither the king nor his attendants showed any signs of **fear or repentance** at what they heard."* (Jeremiah 36:23-24). They did not rend their garments and bow down in sackcloth and ashes, as was customary when such a word was given by the Lord. They had no intentions of repenting and obeying God, so they cut up the scroll and burned it.

A response like this leads one to question why they even declared a fast if they had no intentions of obeying God's instructions. What was the purpose of King Jehoiakim's fast? He wanted relief from Babylonian oppression but was unwilling to accept it on God's terms. God's terms meant he would have to acknowledge his sins and repent. Clearly, this was not the intent of his fasting. He had no intention of confessing and repenting. All he wanted was for God to save them from the Babylonians, so when Jeremiah prophesied the opposite of what he expected, he rejected the prophecy.

The interesting thing in Jeremiah's prophecy is that God said He would spare them if they repented, but the king rejected the very thing that would have brought him the answer that he so desperately needed. His fasting was not genuine; he was just going through the motions of a ritual that he barely understood, and when the answer came, he did not recognize it.

How many times have we rejected God's answer because it was different from what we expected? Maybe we pray to God for healing, but he tells us to forgive someone, or He highlights sinful practices in our lives. Our goal should be to close off all access points for the enemy more than we want our healing or breakthrough.

If we receive healing or the answers to our prayers without correcting the motives of our hearts, the enemy will continue to afflict us. Therefore, it is important to accept God's instructions, no matter how difficult they may be.

Gods Response

The Lord told Jeremiah and Baruch to rewrite the scroll and, this time, to add an extra judgment that was not there before. *"Get another scroll and write everything again just as you did on the scroll King Jehoiakim burned. Then say to the king, 'This is what the Lord says: You burned the scroll because it said the king of Babylon would destroy this land and empty it of people and animals. Now, this is what the Lord says about King Jehoiakim of Judah: He will have no heirs to sit on the throne of David. His dead body will be thrown out to lie unburied—exposed to the day's heat and the night's frost. I will punish him and his family and his attendants for their sins. I will pour out on them and on all the people of Jerusalem and Judah all the disasters I promised, for they would not listen to my warnings."* (Jeremiah 36:28-31). So the king brought about a worse judgment than before because he refused to repent and seek God's mercy.

It is impossible to reject the instructions of the Lord without further judgment. Have you ever rejected God's instructions and had to fight tougher battles as a result? If we want things to go well in our lives, we should fear God and keep his commandments. However, there may be times in our lives when we fail to keep his commandments, but God extends grace and forgiveness through repentance even when we break his laws.

Grace gives us time to repent, while forgiveness puts an end to our reproach so that we can be at peace with God. If Jehoiakim had accepted God's response and repented, the narrative of the story would be completely different.

Call to Action

Many people today react similarly to the King's reaction when they receive an unexpected answer from God. People dislike hearing about their behavior or that judgment is coming. They refused to accept what God said as an answer because that's not what they wanted to hear.

Many people find themselves in traumatic circumstances they are in because of their actions. They turn blind eyes and deaf ears to the truth that God wants them to hear, which was the only thing that could set them free from those circumstances and spare them from judgment. Fasting without repentance means nothing to God. Sometimes repentance is all it takes to get our breakthroughs. Therefore, we must allow God to convict us of sin and be humble enough to repent.

So as you fast and pray today, remember that sometimes you will not like God's answer, but you should not ignore it. Disregarding God's message to you will not make it go away. He is God and will do what He says He will do if you do not repent. If you break His commandments and He convicts you, humble yourself and ask for forgiveness. Despite your mistakes, he loves you more than you can imagine and wants to forgive you more than you want to be forgiven.

PROMISE: *And it shall come to pass that whoever calls on the name of the Lord Shall be saved. For in Mount Zion and in Jerusalem there shall be deliverance, As the Lord has said, Among the remnant whom the Lord calls."* (Joel 2:32).

17

Ezekiel Fast

"Now get some wheat, barley, beans, lentils, millet, and emmer wheat, and mix them together in a storage jar. Use them to make bread for yourself during the 390 days you will be lying on your side. Ration this out to yourself, eight ounces of food for each day, and eat it at set times. Then measure out a jar of water for each day and drink it at set times." (Ezekiel 4:9-11 NLT).

The Ezekiel fast is one of the most interesting fastings in the Bible. It is so unique that many people don't even consider it fasting. Ezekiel did not voluntarily fast as we are choosing to do today; neither was He fasting to repent for the sins of his people. He was fasting because God commanded him to do it. God also told him that the people would not repent. So why was this fasting necessary? What was the outcome of this fast? Ezekiel's fast was a prophetic fast that was an enactment of pending judgment.

Prophetic Enactment

Whenever God wants people to repent, he will go to extraordinary lengths to get their attention. Almost all of Ezekiel's prophecies are accompanied by some kind of prophetic enactment. In this prophecy,

God wanted to use Ezekiel's fasting as a prophetic sign to the people of Israel that a severe famine was coming.

Some people do not think of this enactment as fasting, but Ezekiel's diet was severely restricted for over a year, and it fits perfectly within both the partial and intermittent fasting categories. He had no meats, sweets, wine, or pleasant bread. It was almost like a Daniel fast, except that Ezekiel was restricted to eating specific portions at set times. And he could only eat the peculiar bread and water God prescribed.

God told him that the purpose of this prophetic enactment was to demonstrate the famine that would take place during the siege. *"Then he told me, "Son of man, I will make food very scarce in Jerusalem. It will be weighed out with great care and eaten fearfully. The water will be rationed out drop by drop, and the people will drink it with dismay. Lacking food and water, people will look at one another in terror and waste away under their punishment."* (Ezekiel 4:16-17). So you see, Ezekiel was prophetically fasting to demonstrate the severity of the impending famine.

Ezekiel Bread

God told Ezekiel to make bread from wheat, barley, beans, lentils, millet, and emmer wheat. Unlike the versions we find in the grocery store today, this bread was not designed to be pleasant. According to God's directions, it was to be prepared like barley cakes, which meant it was dry and tasteless. Yet it had many health benefits for Ezekiel as he laid on his side for a total of 430 days, unable to consume anything but this dry, hard, tasteless, unpleasant bread. Wheat provides energy; barley provides fiber; lentils and beans provide protein; millet provides vitamins; and Emmer wheat provides protein and fiber.

God told Ezekiel to bake it over human dung, but he protested, so God permitted him to use cow dung instead. The Lord could have kept Ezekiel alive without the bread during those days, but he chose this method to demonstrate that His people would eat defiled bread during their exile. *"Then the Lord said, "This is how Israel will eat defiled bread in the Gentile lands to which I will banish them!"* (Ezekiel 4:13). God told Ezekiel to eat measured portions of the bread and drink the measured amounts of water at set times each day.

Eat the Scroll

Interestingly, before Ezekiel fasted, God gave him a scroll and told him to eat it. *"Son of man, listen to what I say to you. Do not join them in their rebellion. Open your mouth and eat what I give you." "Then I looked and saw a hand reaching out to me. It held a scroll"* (Ezekiel 2:8-9). *"So I opened my mouth, and he fed me the scroll. "Fill your stomach with this," he said. And when I ate it, it tasted as sweet as honey in my mouth. Then he said, "Son of man, go to the people of Israel and give them my messages.* (Ezekiel 3:2-4). Although it tasted sweet in Ezekiel's mouth, the message was anything but pleasant. When the scroll was unrolled, Ezekiel said, both sides were covered with funeral songs, words of sorrow, and pronouncements of doom. (Ezekiel 2:10).

The Lord told Ezekiel, *"Son of man, let all my words sink deep into your own heart first. Listen to them carefully for yourself."* (Ezekiel 3:10). God wanted Ezekiel to understand that these words were for not just for the nation but him as well. You see, before we can be a messenger of God to other people, we must first receive the message of God for ourselves. When we feed on the message of God for ourselves, we are less likely to sin against God. If the Lord didn't feed Ezekiel with the scroll, he could have been tempted to participate in Israel's rebellion.

Some years ago, I had an encounter with Jesus in a vision. I was in a cottage, and He gave me something to eat that looked like a potato chip. It melted into my entire body when I put it in my mouth. Then He told me, "Today, we are going to ride down the path of unforgiveness." As we rode down the path, we came under a canopy of trees. The trees had some beautiful pungent smelling fruit on them. I asked the Lord what they were. He said those are the fruit of offense. I turned my nose at them, thinking I would never eat those fruits. Jesus read my thoughts and said, *"If I did not feed you back at the cottage, you would eat them."* God preserved me from eating the bait of offense when I didn't even know to guard against it.

Eating God's scroll will prevent us from eating fruits of offense, rebellion, and all other tempting fruits that the enemy might use to tempt us. As watchmen on the wall, we cannot participate in everything other people do because we must stand out from the crowd to be the light.

Another interesting thing about eating the scroll was that Ezekiel had to eat the whole scroll. He couldn't eat the parts he wanted and left out the parts he didn't want. When we read the bible, we tend to leave out the parts that we don't like and only embrace the parts that we like. That is why some of us, as Christians, live such powerless lives. We need to eat, digest, regurgitate, and meditate on the entire scroll because only then can we hear the whole truth and guard against deception.

A Prophet Among Them

God told Ezekiel I am sending you to a rebellious people. *"And whether they listen or refuse to listen—for remember, they are rebels—**at least they will know they have had a prophet among them**"* (Ezekiel 2:5). In other words; God was saying I know they will not listen, but I want you to be my witness that I warned these people. Remember, God, will do nothing on the earth unless he reveals it to His servant, the prophets, because He will not leave himself without a witness.

Since many prophets warned of the same thing during those days, but the people ignored them, God told Ezekiel to enact the prophecy. So he told Ezekiel, *"Now lie on your left side and place the sins of Israel on yourself. You are to bear their sins for the number of days you lie there on your side."* (Ezekiel 4:4). The will of God for Ezekiel was to fast a day for every year that Israel and Judah sinned. He was bearing the nation's sins as he laid down on one side for 390 days for Israel and 40 days on the other for Judah.

This was a tremendous sacrifice that Ezekiel had to make, but he couldn't do it without the help of God. God told him, *"I will tie you up with ropes so you won't be able to turn from side to side until the days of your siege have been completed."* (Ezekiel 4:8). Those ropes serve to help Ezekiel accomplish God's will. Some things that appear as restrictions are only there to help us accomplish God's will.

Another thing to remember was that Ezekiel was not fasting because of his sins but because he was obedient to God's will. This was a prophetic enactment of what it looks like for one man to take upon himself the sins of the entire nation. Many years later, we see what Ezekiel's enactments represent when Jesus took the world's sins upon himself and chose to be nailed to the cross. Just like Ezekiel was tied up and restrained to the ground, Jesus was nailed to a cross. He was restrained on the cross until He fully bore the punishment for the sins of the world.

Put a Mark on My People

Initially, it may appear that Ezekiel's fasting had no outcome because the people still ended up in captivity after all that fasting. It is only when we get to Ezekiel 9 that we see the result of Ezekiel's fast when God told the angels to *"Walk through the streets of Jerusalem and put a mark on the foreheads of all who weep and sigh because of the detestable sins being committed in their city." Then I heard the Lord say to the other men, "Follow him through the city and kill everyone whose forehead is not marked. Show no mercy; have no pity! Kill them all—old and young, girls and women and little children. But do not touch anyone with the mark. Begin right here at the Temple." So they began by killing the seventy leaders."* (Ezekiel

9:4-6). The people who weep over the sins being committed most likely refer to people who fasted, prayed, and wept as was customary when praying for the sins of the nation.

God eventually reconciled Israel to Him, but because they didn't repent, He couldn't pardon them; they had to bear the consequences of their sins. God spared only the people who were weeping over the sins of the nation while many others died, and the nation eventually went into captivity. Our cries and prayers against sin and injustices distinguish us from those who tolerate it. Therefore we must refuse to tolerate sin in every aspect of our lives.

Call to Action

When we watch what's happening in our nation and around the world, we must cry out against sin. We cannot sit back in a corner and tolerate perversion, violence, injustice, greed, and witchcraft. If you are a child of God, it should make your blood boil when you witness evil. If we tolerate evil, it eventually becomes a part of us.

As we look around the world today, every sin Israel committed is being committed in our times, idolatry, witchcraft, perversions, violence, and crimes. He was restrained on the cross until He fully bore the punishment for the sins of the world.

So as you fast today, set your heart and mind to fast as long as God gives you the grace and in the manner that God wants you to fast. You may not have something specific to fast for, but if you weep over the things that break God's heart, you may spare your own life. Ask the Lord if there is something in your family, nation, or church that you need to fast and pray for. Fast in obedience to His guidance, and you will see supernatural results.

Promise: *"And it shall come to pass afterward That I will pour out My*

Spirit on all flesh; Your sons and your daughters shall prophesy, your old men shall dream dreams, your young men shall see visions. (Joel 2:28).

18

Esther Fast

"When Mordecai learned all that had happened, he tore his clothes, put on sackcloth and ashes, and went out into the midst of the city. He cried out with a loud and bitter cry. And in every province where the king's command and decree arrived, there was great mourning among the Jews, with fasting, weeping, and wailing; and many lay in sackcloth and ashes. So, Esther's maids and eunuchs came and told her, and the queen was deeply distressed. Then she sent garments to clothe Mordecai and take his sackcloth away from him, but he would not accept them." (Esther 4:1, 3-4).

Have you ever heard some distressing news that immediately caused you to break down and cry? The Jews were living in Persia when a death decree was issued against them. Mordecai was the first to learn about this murderous plot. For Mordecai, this might have been like déjà vu. Since he was part of the original exiled group, he knew what it was like to be hunted and killed. (See Esther 2:6). Most likely, he remembered the terror of seeing his people captured, slaughtered, or taken in exile. He knew that a decree from the king was no idle threat, so this death decree was very alarming to him.

Mordecai knew God could deliver His people even if they were living in exile, but he knew that they needed to fast and pray. Mordecai knew how to touch the Heart of God through fasting and prayer. Mordecai didn't have a prophetic word, but he had a problem. So he humbled himself in sackcloth and ashes and desperately cried out to God to deliver his people.

The whole Jewish population living in Persia joined in the fast when they heard about the death decree. Some lay in sackcloth and ashes, while others wept and wailed in the streets. They were already exiled and living in terrible distress, and now a madman wanted to kill them all. So what caused this terrible decree to be sent out against them?

Death Decree

This terrifying situation began *when Haman saw that Mordecai would not kneel down or pay him honor, he was enraged. Yet having learned who Mordecai's people were, he scorned the idea of killing only Mordecai. Instead, Haman looked for a way to destroy all Mordecai's people, the Jews, throughout the whole kingdom of Xerxes.* (Esther 3:5). Mordecai was distressed when he learned about Haman's wicked scheme and even more distressed to know he was the cause of it.

When Haman devised his evil plan to slaughter all the Jews, he sought the king's consent since only a king's edict could achieve such a large-scale genocide. He even bribes the King with money to commit genocide. Haman told *King Xerxes, "There is a certain people dispersed among the peoples in all the provinces of your kingdom who keep themselves separate. Their customs differ from all other people's, and they do not obey the king's laws; it is not in the king's best interest to tolerate them. If it pleases the king, let a decree be issued to destroy them, and I will give ten thousand talents of silver to the king's administrators for the royal treasury." So, the king took his signet ring from his finger and gave it to Haman, son of Hammedatha, the Agagite, the enemy of the Jews. "Keep the money," the king said to Haman, "and do with the people as you please."* (Esther 3:8-11)

Haman told the king that all the people refused to obey the king's law and that their customs were different. It was not wrong for the Jews to practice a different culture because they were forced to live in an unfamiliar culture. But it wasn't the way of life for the Jews or the cultural differences that bothered Haman; it was his ego. Mordecai refused to bow to him, and he thought it was too small a punishment to kill just one Jew, so he plotted to murder them all. So who is this Haman? Why did he have so much influence with the king?

Haman came on the scene after Esther became queen and Mordecai uncovered a plot to assassinate the king. *"After these events, King Xerxes honored Haman, son of Hammedatha, the Agagite, elevating him and giving him a seat of honor higher than that of all the other nobles. All the royal officials at the king's gate knelt down and paid honor to Haman, for the king had commanded this concerning him, but Mordecai would not kneel down or pay him honor."* (Esther 3:1-2). Even though it's unclear why the king accorded Haman such high honor, it explains why he agreed to his evil scheme. Haman had the highest seat of honor among the king's nobles, and everyone bowed to him. The king trusted his judgments and followed his advice.

The king, therefore, allowed him to use his signet ring to issue the death decree. Haman sent the death decree to all the king's provinces with the order to annihilate all the Jews on the thirteenth day of Adar and to plunder their possessions. Haman knew that the decree could not be reversed once he sent the decree in the king's name. This reminds me of the death decree of sin. The Bible says the soul that sins will die. There is no way to get around it, but the good news is that another decree was made on our behalf.

Haman didn't understand that the Jewish people had a secret weapon that was more powerful than the king's decree. He didn't know that fasting and prayer would move the heart of the living God or that this living God fights for his beloved people.

Refuse Comfort

Mordecai initiated the secret weapon of fasting because he was intent on obtaining divine intervention. Although all Jews were fasting, Mordecai was under a special burden for two main reasons. First, the problem originated because he refused to bow, and second, he had inside connections to the palace. King Ahasuerus was the only one who could eliminate the death threat against the Jews. Mordecai had access to Queen Esther, and Queen Esther had direct access to the king.

So Mordecai tore his clothes, put on sackcloth and ashes, and wept in the streets, *"He went as far as the front of the king's gate, for no one might enter the king's gate clothed with sackcloth."* (Esther 4:2). Queen Esther was distressed when she heard Mordecai was wearing sackcloth and ashes and sent him clothes, but he refused to take them. (See Esther 4:4). He refused to take comfort; he remained focused on seeking God's intervention; he was determined to fast until God answered his prayer.

In times of distress, people may try to comfort you, but they don't always understand your pain. Despite their best efforts, only God can relieve and comfort us from our pain. Sometimes we allow temporary comforts to rob us of the passion for pursuing God's intervention. Mordecai didn't want clothes; he needed a move from God; he was interested in the king's ears rather than the king's clothes. He needed the king's favor to cancel the death decree against his people, so he refused to be comforted by the queen's clothes. Sometimes we must refuse to be comforted by earthly things to gain heaven's answers.

In response to Mordecai's refusal to be comforted, Esther sent one of her eunuchs to investigate what was ailing him. If Mordecai had taken the clothes, Esther would not have inquired further about the matter, and many lives would have been lost. Esther's inquiry into the problem allowed Mordecai to explain the situation to Queen Esther.

Mordecai told the Eunuch to instruct Esther to ask the king for mercy for the Jewish people. However, Esther also faced a dilemma because the king had not called her to his presence for thirty days, and she could not go to his presence without being summoned. She instructed the Eunuch to tell Mordecai that she could die if she entered the king's presence without being called. Mordecai's response served as the prophetic word of the Lord. He told Esther, *"If you remain silent, relief and deliverance for the Jews will come from another place, but you and your father's family will perish." And who knows but that you have come to your royal position for such a time as this?"* (Esther 4:14). Notice that God didn't send a prophet, but he released the prophetic word through Mordecai. Sometimes the prophetic word you need will come through you, *for you can all prophesy.* (See 1 Corinthians 14:31)

If I perish

Mordecai conveyed enough desperation to Esther to spring her into action. Esther replied to Mordecai: *"Go and assemble all the Jews who can be found in Susa, and fast for me. Do not eat or drink for three days, night or day, and I and my maidens will fast as you do. After that, I will go to the king, even though it is against the law, and if I perish, I perish!"* (Esther 4:15-16). The people fasted, wept, and mourned for three days. They did not eat or drink because they were desperate to touch the heart of God. The queen also fasted with her maidservants and went before the king uninvited, despite knowing she could die. She initially wanted Mordecai to remain silent and remove his fasting clothes, but she became desperate enough to risk her life to save the lives of her people.

Approaching the King

The King extended the scepter to Esther and told her she could have up to half the kingdom. Despite knowing she could receive up to half of the kingdom, Esther took her time to prepare her request and presented it to the king with great care. She hosted a banquet for the king before she made her request.

One of the keys to successful fasting is worship and thanksgiving. When you express love and gratitude to God for all the blessings you have already received, it touches the heart of God. We sometimes rush into God's presence with our laundry list of desires without setting the table for Him. Let's take a moment to reflect on the way you approach God during prayer and fasting. Do you prepare a banquet for Him with your praise and worship? Do you come to Him in reverence or simply ask for what you want and stop praying? Do you thank Him for the blessings He has already provided for you? We must always *enter His gates with thanksgiving and into His courts with praise. Be thankful unto Him and bless His name* (Psalm 100:4).

Esther wanted to touch the heart of the king, so she prepared a two-day banquet for him. On the second day of the feast, Esther finally made her request to the king, *"If I have found favor with you, your majesty, and if it pleases you, grant me my life—this is my petition. And spare my people—this is my request, for my people and I have been sold to be destroyed, killed, and annihilated. If we had merely been sold as male and female slaves, I would have kept quiet because no such distress would justify disturbing the king.* (Esther 7:3-4). Esther's request was granted, Haman's evil plot was exposed, and they hung him on his own gallows. Since they could not withdraw the evil decree, a new one was written in its place that saved the Jewish nation from total annihilation. Again this reminds me of the new decree that the death and resurrection of Jesus made for us. By the decrees of our sins, we should die, but by the decree of the blood of Jesus, we will live and not die and declare the works of the Lord. And just like the Jewish people had to fight for their lives, we must fight against the decree of death to receive the decree of life.

Mordecai used the most effective method he knew to quickly get

God's attention. Although he didn't receive a prophetic word to initiate his fast, fasting yielded prophetic instructions that saved the entire population. He kept fasting and calling on The Lord until God delivered them from the wicked threat of genocide. Mordecai's refusal to bow to Haman led to the death decree, but God used it to remind the Jewish people that He was still with them and was still willing to fight for them even in exile.

Call to Action

Many situations can cause mourning and weeping, including the death of a loved one, acts of violence, spiritual warfare, and terminal illnesses. Our time of distress should cause us to genuinely seek The Lord, but many people do not turn to Him because they believe He is punishing them. The Lord only allows hardships in our lives to get our attention so that we can repent, fast, and pray. The more the devil unleashes his attacks against us, the more we should fervently seek to touch the heart of God through fasting and prayer.

As you fast and pray today, do you have something in your life, home, family, or nation that causes you distress? Are you sincerely praying about it? You may not have a death decree sent out against your nation, but have you or your loved ones received a terminal diagnosis from your doctor? Fast and pray, and earnestly seek God's answers to your situation.

Be like Mordecai and refuse to allow temporary comforts to keep you from praying until you receive your answers. Be like Esther and prepare a banquet of praise and thanksgiving before making your request. And be aware that the prophetic instructions you seek may come through your spirit as God can speak through just as well as He speaks through anyone else.

PROMISE: *Then you shall call, and the Lord will answer; You shall cry, and He will say, 'Here I am.'* (Isaiah 58:9).

19

Ezra Fast

"Then I proclaimed a fast there at the river of Ahava, that we might humble ourselves before our God, to seek from Him the right way for us, our little ones, and all our possessions. For I was ashamed to request of the king an escort of soldiers and horsemen to help us against the enemy on the road because we had spoken to the king, saying, 'The hand of our God is upon all those for good who seek Him, but His power and His wrath are against all those who forsake Him.' So, we fasted and entreated our God for this, and He answered our prayer." (Ezra 8:21-23).

Have you ever felt like you are a target for the enemy? Could it be that it is because of the treasure you possess inside? We don't understand who we are and what we possess. The enemy knows that we are carrying valuable resources, and the enemy would like nothing less than to rob us of our treasure.

In Ezra's situation, the seventy-year Babylonian exile was over, and King Cyrus released them from exile to return to Jerusalem, just like the prophet Isaiah predicted. They were bringing back the gold articles of Solomon's temple, a large amount of money, and other valuables to restore the temple. Ezra was responsible for safely transporting those valuable possessions to Jerusalem. He didn't want to ask the king to send soldiers with them because he told the king that God would protect those who feared Him. He knew he would pass through dangerous regions and could become enemy targets because of the large amount of valuables in their possession. Ezra decided to take the journey even though it was dangerous to do so without military protection. Let's explore Ezra's fast to understand how he successfully touched the heart of God through fasting.

Enemy Target

Ezra was about to embark on a 900-mile journey from Babylon to his homeland in Jerusalem. Besides the considerable amount of valuable articles of gold and silver, he also had several women and children traveling with them. They were about to travel through the open countryside. They could face attacks by bandits and outlaws along the way and had no weapons to defend themselves. Besides being at risk of being attacked by bandits, the journey also exposed them to harsh climatic conditions. They traveled by wagons, horses, or camels through unpaved roads, deserts, hills, and valleys to reach their destinations. The journey involved crossing rivers and traveling under the scorching desert sun. To endure a journey like that and arrive safely at their destination with all the possessions they were carrying would require supernatural protection.

Ezra considered asking the king for soldiers to guard them along the way but decided to call a fast instead. He knew this was the fulfillment of prophecy. He knew that if God said it, he would perform it. So his confidence was not in military might but in God's ability to protect him and the people traveling with him. Ezra knew they would be protected if they could touch God's heart with his fasting and prayers. So Ezra prayed and asked God to show him the right way for him and the people to travel with all their possessions.

Trust in God

Ezra fasted because the situation required him to trust God beyond his rational comprehension. He knew that traveling to Jerusalem with vast amounts of gold and silver would be a tremendous risk. He was fully aware of the possibility of dangers along the way; he had no military escorts, but he trusted in the Name of the Lord as King David did when he faced Goliath. David told Goliath, *"You come to me with a sword and a spear, but I come to you in the Name of the Lord."* (1 Samuel 17:45). The journey to Jerusalem was Ezra's Goliath, but he chose to trust in the name of the Lord rather than the king's military escort.

Sometimes you will face situations in your life that force you to trust God beyond your natural comprehension. Franklin D. Roosevelt puts it best when he says, "Courage is not the absence of fear, but rather the assessment that something else is more important than fear." You may have to embark on a risky venture, and sickness or danger may threaten your life, but something else is more important than the fear you feel. Like Ezra and David, you can trust confidently in the Name of the Lord. Ezra knew that if you earnestly fast, pray, and seek God's protection, He would hear and answer your prayers.

Although Ezra did not know how God would protect him, he believed He would. Sometimes we don't trust God because we don't know how God is going to do it. God has multiple ways of protecting his people. He can turn the enemy swords against each other, rain, hailstones, or fire, form laws that protect, etc. Trust means we don't know how, but we know who. When you know God, you will confidently trust Him, even though you don't know how.

Ezra chose to trust God confidently on the journey to Jerusalem. Sometimes we must be willing to say yes to the journey, although we know there is opposition along the way. Never allow the enemy to intimidate you away from the will of God. To succeed in your journey, you must trust God confidently and be determined to do what He wants you to do, just like Ezra did.

God honors us when we choose to trust him because He said, in Isaiah 49:23, *"Those who hope in me will not be disappointed.* And Romans 10:11 says, *"Anyone who trusts in him will never be put to shame."* God will not disappoint you or allow you to be put to shame and disgrace if you trust confidently in Him to protect and guide you. Although we know God will protect us, we often turn to the world's system for protection.

World's Protection

Who or what do you turn to for protection when you face difficulties? Is it able to protect you? Sometimes it may take a while to see the manifestation of God's protection, so we often turn to the king's soldiers or the world system for protection instead of turning to God in fasting and prayer. Some people trust medical science, people, or money more than God's ability to heal them.

I heard a testimony of a lady who was praying about taking the COVID vaccine. She was being coerced by her doctor that she needed to take it, but she told him she would pray about it first. As she prayed, the Lord asked her, "What could the COVID vaccine do for her that He couldn't do for her?" She knew not to put her trust in a vaccine, but to put her trust in God.

The world's protection system is only effective when it's in the hands of God. God can use the world's systems to protect us, but we must ask Him which system He wants us to use. When we allow God to show us how and when to use natural protection, supernatural things happen. Never allow the world's system of protection to take precedence over God's supernatural protection. Always seek God's protection through prayer and fasting, and allow Him to show you the right path and when to take it.

God's Protection

I was scheduled for surgery some time ago, but I felt led to fast and pray about it in the weeks leading up to surgery, and when I arrived at the hospital, my doctor was called away on an emergency. It turned out that I did not need surgery but had to undergo a lesser procedure that gave me the same results as surgery. Medicine and science are beneficial to us, but there are risks in some medical treatments. We need God's direction when undertaking a risky situation, but we can only find out if we do what Ezra did — fast and pray for God's direction and protection.

Rather than cowering in fear as he faced danger, Ezra chose to trust God's protection through fasting and prayer. Hebrews 10:39 says, *"But we do not belong to those who shrink back and are destroyed, but to those who have faith and are saved.* Because Ezra had faith in the great big God He served; he did not shrink back in fear or ask the king for military protection.

Fulfillment of Prophecy

One of the main reasons for Ezra's successful fasting was the return of the exiled was a fulfillment of prophecy. According to Jeremiah 29:10-12, *This is what the Lord says: "When seventy years are completed for Babylon, I will come to you and fulfill my good promise to bring you back to this place. For I know the plans I have for you," declares the Lord, "plans to prosper you and not to harm you, plans to give you hope and a future. Then you will call on me and come and pray to me, and I will listen to you."* Ezra knew that he was standing in the fulfillment of this prophecy, and he also knew that God would grant him his request for protection. So Ezra confidently requests the Lord's protection.

Ezra's God is the same God we serve today, and He is still interested in keeping His prophetic promises to us today. The same protection Ezra received is available to us if you decide to do what he did.

Call to Action

Sometimes, the things God has tasked us to do will be difficult and dangerous, but we must trust him to help us get them done. Many people surrender in fear when faced with difficulties and danger, but some fast and pray.

If you are facing something difficult or dangerous and you need direction or protection from the Lord, seek Him with fasting and prayer, and He will direct and protect you. When God's hand of protection is upon you, He protects you from everything, including things you can and cannot see.

I do not know what my surgery results would have been had I went through with it, but I felt God protected me from something I could not see. He is constantly protecting us from dangers we cannot see, so we must trust Him to protect us from the ones we see. Nothing touches the heart of God like trusting in Him completely.

So as you fast to seek God's divine guidance and protection as Ezra did, He will certainly hear and answer your prayers. Talk to God about that thing that you are fearing. He knows you seek to honor Him by not shrinking back in fear, so He will quickly respond to you.

Also, keep in mind that sometimes it may take a while for your answer to manifest, but don't give up; continue to trust Him to guide and protect you, and He will preserve your life.

PROMISE: *The Lord will guide you continually, satisfy your soul in drought, and strengthen your bones; you shall be like a well-watered garden and like a spring of water whose waters do not fail.* (Isaiah 58:11).

20

Nehemiah Fast

"And they said to me, 'The survivors who are left from the captivity in the province are there in great distress and reproach. The wall of Jerusalem is also broken down, and its gates are burned with fire.' So it was, when I heard these words, that I sat down and wept and mourned for many days; I was fasting and praying before the God of heaven." (Nehemiah 1:3-4).

When Nehemiah heard that the walls and gates of Jerusalem were destroyed, he became distressed and felt compelled to fast and pray. God trusted Nehemiah with the responsibility of helping the Jewish people in distress because he was the ideal person for the job. Nehemiah was the king's cupbearer, and he was favored by the king. I found Nehemiah's fast fascinating because of his prayers and how he approached God. Let's examine how Nehemiah prayed to glean insights from his prayer.

God of Covenant

First, Nehemiah praised God and reminded Him that He is a covenant-keeping God. *"Lord God of heaven, O great and awesome God, you who keep Your covenant and mercy with those who love You and keep Your commandments"* (Nehemiah 1:5). During Nehemiah's prayer, his people were in great distress. Jerusalem's walls were broken down, and the gates were destroyed by fire. So, how could he call God an awesome God? How could he say God keeps His covenant with those who love him? The natural events that were occurring could have easily led Nehemiah to conclude that God has abandoned His people and broken his covenant. Instead, Nehemiah appealed to God's integrity because he knew God is faithful. Nehemiah saw beyond the natural realm and understood that God keeps His covenants from generation to generation. He understood that even though the walls of Jerusalem were broken down and the city was in ruins, God's covenant was still intact.

People often blame God for pain and suffering because they do not see suffering as the effects of sin. They may even ask, "If God loved us so much, why does He allow us to suffer?" We must understand, as Nehemiah did, that sin causes pain and suffering, not God. God is always good. Even His punishments are good because they lead us to repentance. So instead of blaming God, Nehemiah humbled himself by repenting and confessing his and people's sins. (See Nehemiah 1:6-7).

Confessed Sins

The next thing Nehemiah did was confess the sins of the people because he knew they were in great distress because they violated God's commands. He reminded God of the prophetic words He gave Moses, *"Remember, I pray, the word that You commanded Your servant, Moses, saying, 'If you are unfaithful, I will scatter you among the nations; but if you return to Me, and keep My commandments and do them, though some of you were cast out to the farthest part of the heavens, yet I will gather them from there, and bring them to the place which I have chosen as a dwelling for My name."* (Nehemiah 1:8-9).

Nehemiah understood from reading the Scriptures that God desires His people to repent and return to Him. He repented on behalf of his nation and himself through fasting and prayer. Nehemiah reminded God of his covenant that if His people sin, He will scatter them, but He will bring them home if they repent. God not only heard Nehemiah's prayers, but he answered them quickly.

All it took to move the heart of God was for one righteous man to stand in the gap and intercede for the nation. What would happen if you repented and prayed for the sins of your nation? When we face distress or calamity, we often blame God, but could it be that we face difficulties because of sin issues in our lives? Nehemiah did not blame God in his prayer because he understood God's word; instead, he blamed the people's distress on their sins.

Two Natures

Despite our best efforts, there will be times when we are distressed by the sins that we commit in our lives. Most of our sins are unintentional, while others are intentional. Our fallen world causes us to sin without realizing it, but if we repent when we recognize our sins, the Lord is faithful and righteous to forgive us. As long as you are in this body, you are prone to sin, but God will grant you grace to help you repent. According to Romans 7:21-23, we have two natures, the flesh and the spirit, and they are constantly at war with each other. Thus, we are prone to sin, but the Holy Spirit is perfecting us until Christ returns. Whenever we sin, we must repent and confess our sins as Nehemiah did, and God will quickly answer our prayers.

Sometimes, the Lord allows painful events to help us repent for our sins. But it is also important to remember that God does not condemn us for our sins. We condemn ourselves when we refuse to repent from our sins.

When you sin, be quick to repent and always remember that you have an Advocate with the Father who is pleading your case (1 John 2:1). Also, keep in mind that it's not by works lest we should boast. We received God's forgiveness by grace through faith in Jesus Christ, our Great High Priest, who is always making intercession for us.

Nehemiah Repented for Israel

Nehemiah's pain reminded him that something was wrong. Despite his pleasant life as the king's servant, he was distressed because of the living conditions of the people in Jerusalem. In an effort to lead us to repentance, God will often allow us to go through distressing situations in our families and nation. Therefore, some painful situations in our lives are God's goodness in disguise, leading us to repentance.

Nehemiah continued to pray, *"O Lord, I pray, please let Your ear be attentive to the prayer of Your servant, and to the prayer of Your servants who desire to fear Your name; and let Your servant prosper this day, I pray, and grant him mercy in the sight of this man"* (Nehemiah 1:11). Nehemiah wanted to ask King Darius for permission to travel to Jerusalem. However, he did not know how the king would react, so he prayed to God to grant him favor with the king. The only thing Nehemiah prayed to God for was favor with this king. However, before he made his request, he worshiped God, confessed his sins, and repented.

Not only did God grant him his request, but He gave him more than he asked for. Nehemiah was able to travel to Jerusalem with letters from the king that gave him protection and access to enough resources to rebuild the walls of the city, the temple, and homes for the people to live in. (See Nehemiah 2:6-9). Nehemiah used the world system of protection because it was beneficial to accomplish what needed to be done in Jerusalem. The king's military escort went with him to Jerusalem, and the governors honored the king's letters and gave Nehemiah everything he needed to rebuild the walls and the city gates.

Opposition

Opposition is bound to arise any time you step out in faith to do anything for God. So after Nehemiah had fasted, prayed, and received favor from the king, he went to Jerusalem to rebuild the walls of the city, but Sanballat and Tobiah opposed him. They were very critical and angry that walls were being rebuilt. *"They made plans to come and fight against Jerusalem and throw us into confusion. **But we prayed** to our God and guarded the city day and night to protect ourselves."* (Nehemiah 4:8-9).

I love how Nehemiah responded to the threats because he did not stop the work to engage in a battle that had no rewards. He prayed to the Lord about the situation and posted watchmen to guard the city. We can learn a great lesson from Nehemiah if we respond with prayer and fasting when facing opposition. Often times we backlash and criticize and reduce ourselves to the level of our enemies instead of taking it to God in prayer.

Prayer should be our first line of defense, and when the Lord releases strategies to us in prayer, we should act accordingly. Nehemiah's strategy in facing Sanballat's threats was half the men would work, and the other half would carry swords. They work with a tool in one hand and a weapon in the other. They worked from sunrise to sunset, and half the men were always on guard. (See Nehemiah 4:16-21).

When Sanballat and Tobiah saw that they couldn't stop the work of the Lord, they sent messengers to request a meeting with Nehemiah but he told them, *"I am engaged in a great work, so I can't come. **Why should I stop working to come and meet with you?**"* (Nehemiah 6:3). This is a great example of how we should respond to the enemy, never let the enemy distract you from your purpose.

Nehemiah did not go through all that fasting and prayer or journey all the way to Jerusalem to meet with Sanballat or Tobiah. His mission was to build a wall, and that's what he did. Opposition or no opposition, we need to keep our focus on what the Lord has called us to and not let the enemy's distractions prevent us from fulfilling our God-given purpose.

Despite the opposition, Nehemiah was able to complete the wall in record time. *"So on October 2, the wall was finished—just fifty-two days after we had begun."* (Nehemiah 6:15). There was no doubt that the Lord was with them, and a miraculous work was done. Likewise, when we keep our focus on the Lord's work, we can do all things through Him, who gives us strength. (See Philippians 4:13).

Call to Action

Consider what happens in your family, communities, and nation. Are there some distressing situations that require a move of God? Think about the ungodly laws passed in your nation's government; think about the perversion and idolatry in pop culture. Does it break your heart or see immorality run rampant in your nation? Do you weep over your nation as Nehemiah did? Do you fast and pray over your nation and family?

Only through acknowledging our faults and genuine repentance can we truly humble ourselves and accept God's grace and forgiveness. Let us follow Nehemiah's example of weeping and fasting, worshiping God, confessing and repenting from our sins, and on behalf of our nation. Let's petition the courts of heaven to send deliverance to our families and to our nations. Then follow through with what God has told you to do regardless of what opposition you may face.

So as you fast and pray today, acknowledge anything God has highlighted to you as a sin in your family or nation, confess them before God, and repent from them before making your petitions to Him. Pray for the thing that is burdening the heart of God. God will hear your prayers and grant you His mercy and favor.

PROMISE: *Those from among you shall build the old waste places; you shall raise up the foundations of many generations; and you shall be called the Repairer of the Breach, the restorer of streets to dwell In.* (Isaiah 58: 12)

21

Daniel Fast

"It was the first year of the reign of Darius the Mede, the son of Ahasuerus, who became king of the Babylonians. During the first year of his reign, I, Daniel, learned from reading the word of the LORD, as revealed to Jeremiah the prophet, that Jerusalem must lie desolate for seventy years. So, I turned to the Lord God and pleaded with him in prayer and fasting. I also wore rough burlap and sprinkled myself with ashes." (Daniel 9:1-3).

The Daniel fast is popular among Christians and non-Christians alike, but some have never stopped to consider why Daniel fasted. Daniel was a Jewish man living in Babylonian captivity. He learned from the scrolls of the prophet Jeremiah that God sentenced His people to seventy years of desolation to punish them for their sins. It convicted Daniel so profoundly that he began seeking the Lord through fasting and prayer.

Daniel fasted, prayed, and confessed his sins and the sins of the nation. In Daniel 9:3-6, he said, *"Then I set my face toward the Lord God to request by prayer and supplications, with fasting, sackcloth, and ashes. And I prayed to the Lord my God and confessed, and said, "O Lord, great and awesome God, who keeps His covenant and mercy with those who love Him, and with those who keep His commandments, we have sinned and committed iniquity, we have done wickedly and rebelled, even by departing from Your precepts and Your judgments. Neither have we heeded Your servants, the prophets, who spoke in Your name to our kings and princes, our fathers, and all the people of the land."* Take note of how Daniel approached God in prayer. Rather than just making his request, he reminded God of His sovereignty, and that He is a covenant-keeping God, then he confessed his sins and the sins of his people. Although Daniel did not disclose all that he read in those prophetic scrolls, it was enough to convict him and initiate repentance in his heart. It is important to read and understand the word of God. In order to fully understand the word of God and we cannot pick and choose what parts to read; we must eat the whole scroll.

Eat the Scroll

During the 21 days of fasting that birth this book, The Lord gave us prophetic instructions to eat the whole scroll, meaning that we should read and digest both the hard and easy parts of the scriptures. Christians today pick and choose which parts of the Bible they will apply to their lives, but God wants us to read and digest it all.

Daniel learned through the scrolls that the desolation was because of the sins of the people because he ate the whole scroll. He must have eaten a lot of the less-than-savory parts of God's scroll because he said, *"Every curse written against us in the Law of Moses has come true. Yet we have refused to seek mercy from the LORD our God by turning from our sins and recognizing his truth. Therefore, the LORD has brought upon us the disaster he prepared. The LORD, our God, was right to do all these things, for we did not obey him"* (Daniel 9:13-14). This meant that Daniel not only studied Jeremiah's scroll but also Moses's laws because he said every curse written in the laws of Moses has come upon us, yet we refuse to pray. He was intent on eating the whole scroll because he wanted to find out why they were in this distressing situation and what could be done about it.

From reading the prophetic scrolls, Daniel understood that God warned the people that they would be exiled if they did not repent of their sins. He also understood that God would forgive them if they repented and returned to Him. The prophecies ignited a passion in Daniel's heart to fast, pray, and repent on behalf of his nation. Daniel prayed to God and asked for mercy for his nation and himself.

The word of God can move our hearts to fast and pray for our nation just as Daniel did. When we look around us, we do not have to look very far to see all kinds of pain and suffering. Like Daniel, we need to understand our times and how God's word applies to us now. We need to read the scriptures that apply to our living times and pray them back to God in fasting and repentance. Repentance is the key that unlocks revival. If we want to see revival in our generation, we must start with repentance. We must return to God through fasting, praying, and confessing our sins.

If we never sinned, we would be in harmony with God and would not need to repent. But we have sinned, so we need to repent and come back in right standing with God. Painful situations are sometimes blessings in disguise that lead us to repentance. Daniel recognizes the pain and oppression of his people, but he also recognizes that the people didn't repent. Daniel didn't just routinely fast as we do today; there was purpose in his fasting.

Routine Fast

Many people observe Daniel's twenty-one-day fast each year but do not achieve the results that Daniel did. This is because they rarely pray as Daniel did. Fasting should be motivated by a desire in our hearts that matches the will of God. If you do not fast from your heart, it will not touch the heart of God. If we fast routinely just because it's that time of year, we may as well be dieting to lose weight. Those kinds of fasts do not move the heart of God, but if your goal is losing weight, you certainly will.

A routine fast can be effective if the Holy Spirit or Scripture prompts you to do it. For example, if you need to fast when you read about the day of atonement, do so. If you are fasting because of the new year or because it's the season to fast, you are just performing a meaningless ritual. The Holy Spirit should inspire your fasting, and He can use anything to do so, the scriptures, something you heard or experienced, the season, or a broken heart. I'm not suggesting you shouldn't fast routinely; however, you need to fast with the right motives to get the desired results.

Fair Punishment

Daniel fasted because he recognized that sin was the cause of the distressing situation his nation was in, so he continued his prayer by saying, *"We have sinned and done wrong. We have rebelled against you and scorned your commands and regulations. We have refused to listen to your servants, the prophets, who spoke on your authority to our kings, princes, ancestors, and all the land's people."* (Daniel 9:5-6).

Although the people's punishment was harsh, Daniel recognized God's judgment was just and fair because of their failure to listen to God's servants, the prophets. The People sinned; God sent prophets to warn them, but they refused to repent, so God sent judgment. God always desires repentance from His people because he delights in showing mercy. He does not want to send judgment, but it will come if we refuse to repent.

After repenting profoundly, Daniel made his petition, reminding God of His great love for Israel. *"O Lord our God, you brought lasting honor to your name by rescuing your people from Egypt in a great display of power. But we have sinned and are full of wickedness. In view of all your faithful mercies, Lord, please turn your furious anger away from your city Jerusalem, your holy mountain'"* (Daniel 9:15-16a). As he prayed, he recalled how God miraculously rescued his ancestors from Egypt, but they later turned away from God to worship idols. Daniel recognized that all the judgments were fair and just, but Daniel still pleaded with the Lord for mercy.

Observe how Daniel prayed. All he wanted to ask for was mercy and forgiveness, but he did not approach God without worship and certainly not without godly sorrow over his and his ancestors' sins. His first actions were to worship God, confess his sins, and show godly sorrow over his sins and the sins people's sins before pleading for mercy and forgiveness.

Notice that Daniel did not exclude himself from the sins of his people. We sometimes pray for others but exclude ourselves, believing that others have sinned, but we have not. Daniel included himself in the repentance, and we should do the same when we pray. Genuine fasting and prayer will cause us to recognize our faults and our dependence on God. Then we will begin to sincerely seek the will of God.

God's Response

Daniel was able to successfully touch the heart of God, so much so that the angel Gabriel brought him the answer to his prayers.

> *"I went on praying and confessing my sin and the sin of my people, pleading with the Lord my God for Jerusalem, his holy mountain. As I was praying, Gabriel, whom I had seen in the earlier vision, came swiftly to me at the time of the evening sacrifice. He explained to me, "Daniel, **I have come here to give you insight and understanding.** The moment you began praying, a command was given. And now I am here to tell you what it was, for you are very precious to God. Listen carefully so*

*that you can understand the meaning of your vision. **"A period of seventy sets of seven has been decreed for your people and your holy city to finish their rebellion, to put an end to their sin, to atone for their guilt, to bring in everlasting righteousness, to confirm the prophetic vision, and to anoint the Most Holy Place.** Now listen and understand! Seven sets of seven plus sixty-two sets of seven will pass from the time the command is given to rebuild Jerusalem until a ruler—the Anointed One—comes. Despite the perilous times, Jerusalem will be rebuilt with streets and strong defenses.*

*"After this period of sixty-two sets of seven, **the Anointed One will be killed,** appearing to have accomplished nothing, and a ruler will arise whose armies will **destroy the city and the Temple.** The end will come with a flood, and war and its miseries are decreed from that time to the very end. The ruler will make a treaty with the people for a period of one set of seven, but after half this time, he will put an end to the sacrifices and offerings. And as a climax to all his terrible deeds, **he will set up a sacrilegious object that causes** desecration until the fate decreed for this defiler is finally poured out on him."* (Daniel 9:20-27).

While much interpretation is needed here, it is sufficient to say that Daniel received the answer to his prayers because he simply wanted to know what would happen to his Jewish people. God revealed his master plans for Israel, and I'm sure it gave Daniel great peace to know that although Jerusalem was looking like a wilderness wasteland, God still had a plan. So although we can always see or understand God's plan, we must trust that he has one and is working it out for our good.

Call to Action

Sometimes the answers to your problems are hidden in God's scrolls.

If you don't read the word of God, you won't know what to pray for or how to pray. Prophetic fasting happens when we read His word in its entirety because that's how we find out what God wants us to pray for.

When we fast, God's will should always take precedence over ours. We sometimes think we seek God in prayer when all we seek are solutions to our problems. While we may begin our fast unaware of God's will, if we continue to seek His heart during our fast, the will of God will become more apparent. Once we perceive the will of God in prayer, it's up to us to align our hearts to it and begin praying from that place.

As you fast and pray today, if you want to touch the heart of God as Daniel did, read, and apply the word of God in your praying. Let the word of God convict you and allow the Holy Spirit to guide the direction of your prayers. Whatever challenges we face, we can always find answers in the Bible. Find the scriptures that address your concern, and then pray them back to God.

And remember, the goal of fasting should not be to get as much as possible from God but to desire righteousness, peace, and joy in the Holy Spirit. Your goal is for the kingdom of God to come into your life and for His will to be done on earth as it is in heaven.

PROMISE: *Then you shall delight yourself in the Lord, and I will cause you to ride on the high hills of the earth and feed you with the heritage of Jacob, your father. The mouth of the Lord has spoken."* (Isaiah 58:14).

22

Zechariah Fast

"They were to ask this question of the prophets and the priests at the Temple of the Lord of Heaven's Armies: "Should we continue to mourn and fast each summer on the anniversary of the Temple's destruction, as we have done for so many years?" (Zechariah 7:3)

Sometimes we can become discouraged from fasting and praying, and we may even wonder if we should continue fasting. We may even doubt that God is taking note of our fasting. We may even wonder, are my fasting and prayers making a difference in my life and my nation? Many times we will be tempted to believe nothing is happening when we fast, but God always has a way of confirming His word. Sometimes, we need to stop our routine fasting and prayer ritual to inquire if God really wants us to fast.

This was the case when some men from Bethel came to the prophet Zechariah to ask if they should continue fasting in the summer and fall months. Those fasts represented their mourning for Jerusalem's fall and the temple's destruction. When they came to inquire of the Lord through the Prophet Zechariah, their exile had ended, and the temple rebuilding was underway. However, they were not hearing from God, so they came to inquire from the priest and the prophets.

A successful fast is usually done with God's agenda in focus. When we fast, we do so often because of our desires rather than trying to seek the heart of God. Therefore we will end up questioning whether or not we should continue fasting.

Construction Angels

One morning during our fasting and prayer service, The Lord instructed us to pray for Jerusalem. His agenda that morning was to assign spiritual watchmen to the walls of Jerusalem. The Lord said, "I am placing watchmen in every corner of the world, and they will blow My trumpet and sound My alarm! No one will silence them! Many will try to silence them, but the more they try, the louder the alarms will sound. I desire to show mercy, not judgment, but judgment will certainly come if people refuse to heed the warnings." As I released this prophetic word from the Lord, I saw a vision of angels doing construction work in Jerusalem.

Two angels were measuring and inspecting a freshly laid concrete foundation. One angel had a wheelbarrow, and the other had a measuring tool. Other angels were working at the far end of the construction site. The angels took various measurements of a building under construction and pushed materials around in wheelbarrows.

The Lord said, "A spiritual foundation is being laid in Jerusalem for the Jewish people to return to Me, but many will oppose it, as in the days of Ezra and Nehemiah. Therefore, I am raising watchmen to pray for the peace of Jerusalem. Isaiah 62:6-7 says, *"I have set watchmen on your walls, O Jerusalem; neither day nor night will they hold their peace." You who mention the LORD, do not keep silent, and give Him no rest till He establishes and till He makes Jerusalem a praise in the earth."* So God is inviting people to participate in his holy work in Jerusalem.

Sometime later, I went to a pastor's conference and learned that a well-known pastor was purchasing properties in Israel dedicated to being used to pray for the salvation of the Jews. Instantly I knew that it was the foundation I saw in my vision. Of course, I sowed the largest seed I could to help lay the foundation for God's agenda. We don't really understand the impact that prayer has on the earth. It really is foundational to everything that God does on earth. Therefore we need to understand how to do it right.

So when the people came to ask the prophet, Zechariah, if they should continue fasting, this was good because they wanted to find out what was on God's agenda. They were going through the motions of fasting but were not seeing any results or receiving any prophetic instructions from the Lord. It appears that something was wrong with their foundation because God was not answering their prayers. The people knew that when they fasted, God would bless them, so they used it as a tool to seek favors and blessings from God. They didn't understand that their repentance was the key to fasting that releases the blessings. We often do things because we see other people doing it, and it works, but we do not know why. Fasting without repentance does not touch the heart of God and will cause your foundation of prayer to fail inspection.

The Lord's Response

There is a huge difference between fasting for cleansing and break-throughs and fasting for the Lord. When the people came to the prophet Zechariah to inquire if they should continue fasting. The Lord responded by asking, *'During these seventy years of exile, when you fasted and mourned in the summer and in early autumn, was it really for Me you were fasting? And even now, in your holy festivals, aren't you eating and drinking just to please yourselves?'* (Zechariah 7:5-6). The Lord told them they were fasting to please themselves because they were not really seeking Him. All they wanted was for God to restore

Jerusalem. They were not concerned about returning to God in sincere repentance.

Because the people didn't know why they were fasting, God told them they were eating and drinking to please themselves. In other words, God told the people that they have no real desire to return to Him when they fast; all they want is for the temple to be restored so that they can return to the way things were. They were just going through the motions of fasting so that God would give them what they wanted. They didn't understand that the key element in fasting that releases the blessings of God is repentance. So the Lord gave them the same prophetic instructions that He gave their ancestors.

> "This is what the Lord of Heaven's Armies says: Judge fairly and show mercy and kindness to one another. Do not oppress widows, orphans, foreigners, and the poor. And do not scheme against each other. "Your ancestors refused to listen to this message. They stubbornly turned away and put their fingers in their ears to keep from hearing. They made their hearts as hard as stone, so they could not hear the instructions or the messages that the Lord of Heaven's armies had sent them by his Spirit through the earlier prophets. That is why the Lord of Heaven's armies was so angry with them." (Zechariah 7:9-12).

The Lord told them your ancestors were fasting and praying to Me, but I would not listen to them because they did not listen to Me. He told them if you want Me to listen to you, this is what you should do, follow the instructions I gave your forefathers. God was not interested in another meaningless fast but in repentance.

God wanted the people to return to Him with all their hearts, but they were not fasting for Him. God's love for them is everlasting, and He was yearning for His people, but the empty rituals of fasting with no change of heart were meaningless to Him. God revealed through the prophets that all He wanted was for the people to obey His laws, and He would be merciful and return to them.

Promise to Return

Although their disobedience blocks their flow of blessing, God opened up another channel to bless them. The prophet told them, *"This is what the Lord of Heaven's Armies says: My love for Mount Zion is passionate and strong; I am consumed with passion for Jerusalem!" "And now the Lord says: I am returning to Mount Zion and will live in Jerusalem. Then Jerusalem will be called the Faithful City; the mountain of the Lord of Heaven's Armies will be called the Holy Mountain."* (Zechariah 8:2-3). Although they fasted with the wrong motives, God still released the prophetic message and told them He was returning to Jerusalem and that He would bless them because He was consumed with love for them. He told them He would not treat them as he did their ancestors. *"For this is what the Lord of Heaven's Armies says: I was determined to punish you when your ancestors angered me, and I did not change my mind, says the Lord of Heaven's Armies. But now, I am determined to bless Jerusalem and the people of Judah. So don't be afraid."* (Zechariah 8:14-15 NLT).

God used His love and mercy channel to bless them. He blessed them, not on the merit of their fasting, but simply because He loved them and wanted to be with His beloved people.

So although they were not fasting correctly, God still revealed his prophetic plans for Jerusalem. He did so because He wanted them to confidently trust that He would not change His mind. He wanted them to see past the war-ravaged Jerusalem and see it fully restored and the temple built, and the streets bustling with activities as they once were. He gave them hope for Jerusalem when they were feeling discouraged and had no hope.

The Lord also told them what they should do if they wanted to see

His promises fulfilled, *"But this is what you must do: Tell the truth to each other. Render verdicts in your courts that are just, and that lead to peace. Don't scheme against each other. Stop your love of telling lies that you swear are the truth. I hate all these things, says the Lord."* (Zechariah 8:16-17). So again, the Lord was not as interested in their fasting as he was in their obedience. Fasting only becomes necessary when we break God's commandments. All God wanted them to do was to keep His commandments.

Keeping the commandments was important to God because the Jewish people were intended to be a royal priesthood, a holy nation. They were to represent God to the rest of the nations. They did not represent God well when they broke His commandments. Furthermore, when they disregard God's commandments, they disregard Him. So God told them if they keep His commandments, *"The fasts of the fourth, fifth, seventh, and tenth months will become joyful and glad occasions and happy festivals for Judah. Therefore, love truth and peace."* (Zechariah 8:19). God was telling them, by keeping My commandments, you will successfully touch My heart. I will accept your fast and turn your mourning into dancing.

Call to Action

Our agenda for fasting might be different from God's agenda. Sometimes we fast for selfish purposes rather than pursuing the heart of God. Do not just fast routinely; pause like these people did when they went to the prophet Zechariah to inquire of the Lord. Seek God's agenda, and He will reveal His plans to you.

Many prophecies must be fulfilled in Israel and in the nations before Jesus returns. The foundation of prayer and fasting is being laid to prepare the way of The Lord, but there is great opposition. Therefore, Lord is commissioning watchmen to fast and pray for the peace of Jerusalem and for the nations of the world.

So as you fast and pray today, consider what is on the heart of God for your nation. Are you fasting to please the Lord or to please yourself? Are you obeying His commandments? Is there something that the Lord is telling you to do that will make your fast acceptable to Him?

You will touch the heart of God when you obey His commandments and fast for His agenda. He will reveal His prophetic plans to you as you fast. He will confirm His word in various ways, whether by direct prophecy or through other means. Also, keep in mind that there are many false prophets, so use discerns to determine if a prophetic word is from God or not.

Promise: *"If we are unfaithful, he remains faithful, for he cannot deny who he is."* (2 Timothy 2:13)

23

Fasted Life

"There was also a prophet, Anna, the daughter of Penuel, of the tribe of Asher. She was very old; she had lived with her husband seven years after her marriage and then was a widow until she was eighty-four. She never left the temple but worshiped night and day, fasting and praying." "Coming up to them at that very moment, she gave thanks to God and spoke about the child to all who were looking forward to the redemption of Jerusalem." (Luke 2:36-38).

What does it mean to live a fasted life? Anna was a widow who lived in Jerusalem around the time of Jesus's birth. She worshiped, fasted, and prayed in the temple night and day. We don't know a great deal about Anna's life. As far as we know, she was a widow, about eighty-four years old. After her husband died, she devoted herself to serving God through prayer and fasting in the temple. She did not fast and pray because of distress or danger but because it was her lifestyle. Anna's selfless devotion earned her the respect of those who knew her. Thus, she was regarded as a prophetess at a time when they did not readily regard women as prophetesses.

Led by the Holy Spirit

Anna's lifestyle of fasting and praying in the temple demonstrated selflessness. Anna did not need to fast but did so out of devotion to God. The purpose of devoted fasting is to yield to the Holy Spirit's direction, not to meet a need or respond to distress. The grace of the Holy Spirit is necessary to sustain a fasted lifestyle since our flesh nature opposes fasting. To live a fast life, we need more than willpower; we need the Holy Spirit.

A need or a situation usually motivates us to fast, but when we fast in devotion to God, it touches the heart of God. While there is nothing wrong with fasting out of distress or other circumstances, that should not be our sole motivation. The Holy Spirit can sometimes lead us to fast simply because we love God and desire to please Him.

Anna found purpose in her selfless devotion to fast and pray night and day in the temple because she surrendered her will for God's will. God's will at that time was for someone to fast and pray until the Messiah came, and Anna yielded to that will.

When we don't know God's purpose for our lives, it's hard to surrender our lives to Him selflessly. When we surrender our will to God through fasting, he enables us to understand our purpose and live a life of selfless dedication to Him.

Holiness unto God

Self-denial leads to holiness, which is ultimately what fasting is about, holiness to God. Living holy means living according to God's terms and conditions; fasting enables you to do this. We will experience God's presence more intimately and hear his voice more clearly when we walk in holiness with him. Hearing His voice more clearly will help us understand His will for our lives and helps us to surrender our will to Him completely.

When we yield our will to God, the kingdom of heaven will come to earth through your prayers. In Matthew 6:1, *The Lord Jesus instructed us to pray, "Thy kingdom come; thy will be done on earth, as it is in heaven."* By nature, we are more concerned with our physical desires than spiritual ones, so putting God's will first can be difficult. Fasting and prayer help us suppress the fleshly nature to put God's will first. Fasting helps us find God's will and gives us the grace to fulfill it.

God's Response

Although the Bible does not tell us why Anna fasted in the temple day and night, it is possible she prayed for the Messiah during her lifetime. Her reaction to seeing baby Jesus implied that they somehow related her devotion to prayer and fasting to His birth.

Although we don't know what Anna said about baby Jesus, we can infer from Simeon's prophecy why Anna fasted and prayed because the words she spoke over baby Jesus were in agreement with his prophecy. Simeon prophesied, *"Sovereign Lord, as you have promised, you may now dismiss your servant in peace. For my eyes have seen your salvation, which you have prepared in the sight of all nations: a light for revelation to the Gentiles, and the glory of your people Israel."* Then Simeon blessed them and said to Mary, his mother: *"This child is destined to cause the falling and rising of many in Israel and to be a sign that will be spoken against so that the thoughts of many hearts will be revealed. And a sword will pierce your own soul too."* (Luke 2:29-32, 34-35). When Simeon finished prophesying, Anna entered and began prophesying over baby Jesus. He was just a baby at the time and had not yet performed any miracles, so no one knew who He really was.

In those days, Israel was looking forward to the promised Messiah, so those prophetic words were precious. They were living in a time when the word of God was scarce. The stage was set for the Messiah, but there was no sign of the Messiah. Could this be the reason for Anna's fasting and prayer? Could it be that she devoted her life to fasting and praying for the Messiah to come? Many people have dedicated their lives to prayer and fasting in anticipation of His return as the King of kings and Lord of Lords.

Every Day Fasted Life

You don't have to live in a temple as Anna did to live a fasted life. You can live a fasted life every day while using the gifts and talents God has given you. You can dedicate yourself to fasting and prayer throughout the year by fasting people, places, things, and activities.

The fasted life involves choosing not to indulge in certain pleasures. For example, you might decide not to eat certain foods for your entire life or a season. Many choose not to consume meat, sweets, or other food groups or drink certain beverages for an extended period or even for the rest of their lives. Some people choose to fast from television, vacations, entertainment, and other pleasure activities, while others prefer to live modestly despite having the ability to live in luxury.

Separating yourself from certain people is also an option when trying to live a fasted life. It is sometimes necessary to separate yourself from certain people if they are not moving in the same direction. That is why II Corinthians 6:17 tells us to *"Come out from them and be separate, says the Lord. Touch no unclean thing, and I will receive you."* There was a time in my life when I had to separate from certain people, not because I hated them, but simply because their lifestyle was not conducive to God's presence in mine. I love them, but I could not go where they were going or participate in what they were doing.

A fasted lifestyle could also mean sacrificing your career to consecrate yourself to God. The Lord called me to become a minister while I was in college studying to become a medical doctor. It was challenging to give up my dream of becoming a medical doctor but God's will prevailed over mine. He told me, "The lives you will save as a medical doctor are nothing compared to the lives you will save as a doctor of my word." So, I gave up my desire to become a medical doctor and followed God's call. I had to fast my personal desires to pursue God's desires, and it was the best decision I ever made.

A fasted life could also mean that you choose to remain unmarried in order to devote yourself to God. Many powerful men and women choose to live a fasted life by remaining unmarried, like the Apostle Paul. The decision is challenging, but many people choose to do it. Some struggle with loneliness and other emotions, while others enjoy living a fasted lifestyle. I suspect that the ones who enjoy their fasted lifestyle are the ones who are completely devoted to God. The ones who struggle are looking back over their shoulders wondering what could have been.

This type of fasted life is not for everyone because it is challenging to remain unmarried, which is why the Apostle Paul said in I Corinthians 7:7-9, *"But I wish everyone were single, just as I am. Yet each person has a special gift from God, of one kind or another. So I say to those who aren't married and to widows—it's better to stay unmarried, just as I am. But if they can't control themselves, they should go ahead and marry. It's better to marry than to burn with lust."* The secret to living a fasted life is that the Holy Spirit must lead you.

Call to Action

While we don't know Anna's motivation for fasting for so many years, we can infer from her reaction to baby Jesus that she was praying for the Messiah's arrival. In that case, Anna would have made it her life's mission to fast and pray for the Messiah's arrival. Today our fast is just like Anna's, except that we are not waiting for baby Jesus to come but for the King of Kings and Lord of Lords to come.

So, as you fast today, ask yourself, am I fasting out of devotion and love for God? Why am I fasting? What am I hoping to accomplish through this fast? Is my fasting and prayer in alignment with the will and purposes of God for my life? Am I living a fasted life? Ask God to show you ways that you can live a fasted life.

PROMISE: *Then the LORD will be your delight. I will give you great honor and satisfy you with the inheritance I promised to your ancestor, Jacob. I, the LORD, have spoken!" (Isaiah 58:14).*

24

John the Baptist Fast

"When the prophet John the Baptist came fasting and refused to drink wine, you said, 'He's crazy! There's a demon in him.'" (Luke 7:33).

This is another unusual but very significant fast. It is so unusual that most people do not readily recognize it as a fast because it is not clearly spelled out for us until we read Luke 7:33 when Jesus said, *"John the Baptist came, neither eating bread nor drinking wine, and you say, 'He has a demon.'"* John was not eating bread or drinking wine which sounds similar to what we call a Daniel fast today. Apparently, John the Baptist followed a strict diet of wild honey and locust. (See Matthew 3:4). The Bible doesn't say why he did that but it may have something to do with the Nazirite vow that was prophesied over his life before he was born. Let's explore his life a bit further to understand why John the Baptist fast and why he had to be a Nazirite. When we understand these things, they will help us to fully surrender our lives to God in total devotion to Him.

Angelic Prophecy
John the Baptist's father was a priest named Zechariah who was

burning incense in the temple of the Lord when the angel Gabriel appeared to him and told him he would have a son and he was to name him John. The angel also told Zechariah his son, *"will be great in the eyes of the Lord. He must never touch wine or other alcoholic drinks. He will be filled with the Holy Spirit, even before his birth. And he will turn many Israelites to the Lord their God. He will be a man with the* **spirit and power of Elijah.** *He will* **prepare the people for the coming of the Lord.** *He will turn the hearts of the fathers to their children, and he will cause those who are rebellious to accept the wisdom of the godly."* (Luke 1:15-17).

The interesting thing about this angelic prophecy is that John and his wife were advanced in years, meaning they were past the age of childbearing. So Zechariah questioned the Angel about the prophecy. *"Zacharias said to the angel, "How shall I know this? For I am an old man, and my wife is well advanced in years."* (Luke 1:18). In the natural, this made no sense to Zechariah. It was difficult for Zechariah to understand why the Lord would wait this long to give him a son. And then the tremendous prophecy that he will have the Spirit of Elijah and that he would prepare the way for the coming of the Lord. Zechariah must have thought who am I that such amazing, glorious things should happen to my child? It was incredulous to believe that I could even have a son at this old and even more incredible to believe that he would be chosen to do such amazing things.

So Zechariah was in shock and disbelief. *"And the angel answered and said to him, "***I am Gabriel, who stood in the presence of God** *and was sent to speak to you and bring you these glad tidings. But behold, you will be mute and not able to speak until the day these things take place because* **you did not believe** *my words which will be fulfilled in their own time."* (Luke 1:19-20). Gabriel explained who he was and that he stood in the very presence and God. Zechariah could have said, Gabriel, I don't see you every day, so how would I know who you really are? So the Angel said I'll shut down your voice so that when the prophecy is fulfilled, it will be a sign to you and the people around you.

Sometimes God will tell us things that we can't tell anyone because if you tell them, they will not believe, and sometimes you can't believe it. In cases like those, the best thing to do is to keep your mouth shut when God reveals what he is doing in your life. Cause you see, just because you don't advertise to everyone doesn't mean that God won't fulfill his promise. As the prophet Habakkuk says, sometimes the vision is for an expected time but in the end, it will speak and not lie. So the wonderful thing about this prophecy was that it came true even though Zechariah was not able to speak it into existence.

So just like the Angel predicted, John the Baptist was miraculously conceived, and Elizabeth gave birth to him. Zechariah, who couldn't speak, was suddenly able to speak again, and he prophesied over his son, *"And you, my little son, will be called the prophet of the Most High because you will prepare the way for the Lord. You will tell his people how to find salvation through the forgiveness of their sins."* (Luke 1:76-77). And all of Judea marveled at his miraculous birth.

The prophetic word given by Angel Gabriel to Zechariah had a tremendous influence on the way John the Baptist chose to live his life. Although we didn't get to see much of John's upbringing, we know that he kept the Nazirite vow that was on his life before he was born because the Bible says, *"John grew up and became strong in spirit. And he lived in the wilderness until he began his public ministry to Israel."* (Luke 1:80). His lifestyle was very much influenced by how he came into the world and the fact that he was declared a Nazirite before he was formed in his mother's womb.

Nazirite Vow

Some people choose to do a Nazirite fast while others are born Nazirites. The three basic requirements of a Nazirite vow are; they must abstain from wine and other fermented drinks and not cut their hair or go near a dead body. (see Numbers 6: 2-8). In addition, John the Baptist, Samson, and Samuel were both children that were Nazirites from birth.

An angel appeared to Samson's mother and told her, *do not drink wine or similar drinks and not to eat anything unclean. For behold, you shall conceive and bear a son. And no razor shall come upon his head, for the child shall be a Nazirite to God from the womb; and he shall begin to deliver Israel out of the hand of the Philistines."* (Judges 13:4-5). While Hannah chose to make a vow that if the Lord gave her a child, he would be consecrated to him as a Nazarite. (see Samuel 1)

Many people also choose to do a Nazirite fast to consecrate themselves to God for a certain amount of time and for various reasons. In Acts chapter 18, Apostle Paul shaves his head at Cenchrea, marking the end of a Nazirite vow to the Lord, we don't know what he vowed to the Lord, but it is safe to say he fulfilled his vow. So Nazirites vows were common practice among the Jewish people, whether from birth or by choice. And the interesting thing is when people choose to do a Nazirite fast, God releases His Spirit and power in their lives.

Spirit of Power Elijah

John the Baptist had to be a Nazirite because he was destined to operate in the Holy Spirit as Elijah did. Malachi 4:5-6 prophesied, *"Look, I am sending you the prophet Elijah before the great and dreadful day of the Lord arrives. His preaching will turn the hearts of fathers to their children and the hearts of children to their fathers. Otherwise, I will come and strike the land with a curse."*

I thought about what it meant for John the Baptist to be like Elijah, and two things came to mind; his clothes and his assignment. Well, there is nothing super spiritual about John the Baptist's clothes, but because they resemble the garments that Elijah wore, people would be able to readily identify John as the one coming in the Spirit of Elijah.

"He had a hair garment and a leather belt around his waist." The king said, "That was Elijah the Tishbite." (2 Kings 1:8). So you see, it was not by coincidence that John was dressed in the same apparel as Elijah. Although Elijah was long dead, his apparel was common knowledge among the Jewish people, and John wanted the people to know that the prophecy was being fulfilled.

John, the Baptist's assignment, was similar to that of Elijah because he was chosen to turn the hearts of the children back to the Father. Elijah was able to operate in the power of the holy spirit and successfully turned the hearts of many Israelites back to God at a time when Idolatry and lawlessness were at their peak in the nation. Now John the Baptist was tasked to do the same thing; turn the hearts of the people back to God by preaching repentance to them. In so doing, he would prepare their hearts to receive the long-awaited messiah.

Prepare the way

Seven hundred years before John the Baptist was born, Isaiah prophesied that John the Baptist would come as *the voice of one crying in the wilderness: "Prepare the way of the Lord; Make straight in the desert A highway for our God." (Isaiah 40:3).* During John the Baptist time, it was common for prophets to use the wilderness as a place for preparation for ministry. It represents a place of separation from the world and the influence of the common culture. Remember, even Jesus went to the wilderness to fast and pray before he entered His ministry. I suspect that the same wilderness that Jesus was tempted in was the same one that John was in previously, crying out to prepare the way of the Lord. So John even prepared the wilderness to receive Jesus!

There is something fascinating and enchanting about a wilderness. It reduces you to total dependence on the Lord. We encounter modern-day wildernesses when we go through circumstances in our lives that cause us to come to a place of total dependence on God. Some people choose to go to the wilderness, while others are led to the wilderness by the Holy Spirit. Whatever the case may be, you will find yourself in a spiritual wilderness at some point in your journey but keep in mind the wilderness is a place of testing, and it's temporary. If you understand why you are in your wilderness, you will emerge with great power as John the Baptist and Jesus did.

John understood that he was in the wilderness because he was called to prepare the way of the Lord; therefore, he consecrated himself. Preparing the way of the Lord was more like that of a Herald who would go through the towns and announce the coming of the king or someone of great importance. John the Baptist was Jesus's personal herald; he was sent to announce the appearance of the Lord Jesus Christ. This was to prepare the people to meet the expected Messiah. John's message was, *"Repent of your sins and turn to God, for the Kingdom of Heaven is near.* (Matthew 3:1-2). This was of great significance because the people did not understand their need for a messiah or how to relate to him when he finally came.

So John was tasked with telling the people what to expect when the Messiah arrived. John told them, *"I baptize those who repent of their sins and turn to God with water. But someone who is greater than I am is coming soon—so much greater that I'm not worthy even to be his slave and carry his sandals. He will baptize you with the Holy Spirit and with fire."* (Matthew 3:11). John had to announce the coming of the Lord Jesus because there were false messiahs, and people wouldn't know who was the true messiah without his witness.

So one day, while John was baptizing in the Jordan River, Jesus came to him to be baptized; John introduced Jesus as the Lamb of God that takes away the sins of the world. *"The next day, John saw Jesus coming toward him and said, "Behold! The Lamb of God who takes away the sin of the world!"* (John 1:29).

In those days, the priest was the one who offered lambs to God for the sins of the people. The priest who offered the lamb before the Lord must also be holy, which explains why John the Baptist had to be a Nazirite. The priest must inspect the lamb and then offer it on behalf of the people.

Since John's father, Zechariah was a priest, John was a priest from birth, and a Nazirite, so those two things qualified him to offer the Lamb of God on behalf of the people. But before the Lamb could be offered, three things must happen. Once the Tabernacle had been purified, people must consecrate themselves, and the lamb must be examined since a transition was being made from a physical Tabernacle to a spiritual one. The hearts of people needed to be cleansed, and that was done when people confessed and repented of their sins.

Then John told them to be baptized, which represented the atonement of the sacrificial altar. Then the lamb was inspected for any blemishes. John was also tasked with inspecting and identifying Jesus as the Lamb of God. So God gave him special instructions to look for when inspecting the lamb. *"I didn't know he was the one, but when God sent me to baptize with water, he told me, 'The one on whom you see the Spirit descend and rest is the one who will baptize with the Holy Spirit.' I saw this happen to Jesus, so I testify that he is the Son of God."* (John 1:33-34).

So John completed all the preparations of turning the people's hearts to the Father and identifying Jesus as the son of God. But it was not his job to mail him to the cross, John's job was only to prepare the way, and once that was done, another priest would take over the task of actually making the sacrifice. We saw much later that Caiaphas, the great high priest, was the one who actually turned Jesus over to the Romans to be crucified. (see John 18:38). John did his job so well that Jesus praised him by saying he was the greatest person that was ever born.

I must decrease

John, the Baptist's life, was prophesied years before the angel ever showed up. And he was great in the eyes of the Lord because Jesus said, *"I tell you, of all who have ever lived, none is greater than John. Yet even the least person in the Kingdom of God is greater than he is!"* (Luke 7:28).

To be the forerunner for Jesus means you must be prepared for His appearance. You must help others prepare to meet him too. John chose to live a set apart, consecrated life, and God honored him for that.

Remember, he was not the only Nazirite called from birth because some have corrupted the Nazirite call as Samson did, but John honored his call, and Jesus called him great. In Matthew 9:14, John's disciples once asked Jesus, *"Why don't your disciples fast like the Pharisees, and we do?"* This implies that in addition to John the Baptist's meager diet of locust and wild honey, there was some periodic fasting. So it is safe to say John the Baptist lived a life of fasting, which earned him a reputation for being a great servant of God. But as great a servant as he was, he had his moment of weakness. *"John the Baptist, who was in prison, heard about all the things the Messiah was doing. So he sent his disciples to ask Jesus, **"Are you the Messiah we've been expecting, or should we keep looking for someone else?"*** (Matthew 11:2-3). This was an amazing question coming from the man who declared Jesus to be the Son of God, the Lamb that takes away the sins of the world.

When you go through pain and suffering, it can cause you to question the very existence of God. Because John the Baptist was expecting Jesus to do something about the prison situation, but Jesus did nothing. *"Jesus answered and said to them, "Go and tell John the things which you hear and see: The blind see and the lame walk; the lepers are cleansed, and the deaf hear; the dead are raised up, and the poor have the gospel preached to them **and blessed is he who is not offended because of Me.**"* (Matthew 11:4-6).

This was also a test for John the Baptist and a part of the preparation process because he did not love his life more than he loved Jesus. He came to the place in his heart like many of us do when faced with challenging circumstances, *"He must increase, but I must decrease."* (John 3:30). Even through his pain John remained a faithful ambassador to the Lord.

Call to Action

It is wonderful to know that God has plans for each of us even before we are born. John the Baptist lived an exceptional life because he chose to follow the plans of God for his life. His Nazirite fasted lifestyle is difficult and should not be attempted unless the holy spirit has specifically guided you to do so. However, you can make Nazirite vows as the Lord leads you because He will give you the grace to do whatever he calls you to do. So you may not be a Nazirite, but you can make Nazirites vows of consecration, and remember you don't have to be a male to be Nazirite.

Sometimes a Nazirite fast is easier to do than a periodic fast because it becomes a way of life. As they say, habits are easy to make but hard to break. When choosing to do Nazirite fast, it eventually becomes a lifestyle and easier.

So as you fast and pray today, think about the gift and the calling that are on your life. Are you being faithful to your purpose? Do you become offended at God when your calling takes you to difficult places in your life? Are you willing to decrease so that Christ may increase in you? Ask God to reveal his plans for your life and commit yourself to them, and he will release His Spirit and Power in your life.

Promise: *"For Everyone who calls on the name of the Lord will be saved."* (Romans 10:13)

25

Jesus Fast

Then Jesus was led up by the Spirit into the wilderness to be tempted by the devil, and when He had fasted forty days and forty nights, afterward He was hungry. (Matthew 4:1-2)

Many people fast during the season of Lent for various reasons. Some do so to honor the season, while others do so because the Holy Spirit inspires them. Sometimes you may not understand why the Holy Spirit leads you to fast, but trust Him and do it anyway.

In a true story, a church fasted for nine days despite not knowing why they were under a strong conviction to do so. After nine days of fasting, one member had a demonic encounter that would have ended her life, but the Lord miraculously protected her because the church was fasting. I call those kinds of fast wilderness fast because you feel led to fast but don't know why.

The Holy Spirit led Jesus into the wilderness to fast for forty days, but we were never told why Jesus had to fast. What was the purpose behind Jesus' fasting and prayer? Why was it necessary for Jesus to fast in the wilderness?

Spirit-Led Fasting

Sometimes, the Holy Spirit will lead you to fast without telling you why. The old folks called it an unction to fast and pray. Those Spirit-led fasts are some of the best I've ever done. During these spirit-led fasts, I rarely feel hungry or fatigued. It's almost as if I am not fasting at al,l and that's how you know the Holy Spirit gives you a special grace to fast.

Jesus obeyed the Holy Spirit when He was led to fast in the wilderness. Wilderness symbolizes a place of testing, obscurity, trials, and temptations because they are uncultivated and uninhabited. This represents consecration or disassociation from the influence of common culture. It is almost guaranteed that anyone God chooses to use greatly will go through a wilderness test.

The world was like a wilderness, a wasteland, a spiritually deserted place. Physically, we were alive, but spiritually we were dead. Jesus' mission was to conquer the wilderness of the world and restore humanity to God, but before He could do so, he had to conquer his own wilderness. I call it his wilderness fast or boot camp because it reminds me of soldiers going through boot camp basic training before going to the real battlefield. So what was Jesus doing in the wilderness? Jesus had to pass the three major tests that humanity failed, which caused them to end up in the wilderness of sin. He had to pass; the bread, faith, and love test.

The Bread Test

After fasting for forty days and forty nights, Jesus was extremely hungry. Satan tempted him to make bread out of stones, but Jesus told him, *"Man shall not live by bread alone, but by every word that proceeds from the mouth of God."* (Matthew 4:4). Jesus could easily turn those stones into bread because He is the same Jesus who fed the five thousand from five loaves of bread.

Jesus had to pass the bread test to demonstrate that He was not relying on physical bread but on the word of God to sustain Him through His trials. Jesus could not be the bread of heaven if He relied on the bread of earth for His sustenance.

Many people fail the bread test because they trust the bread more than the bread provider. Adam and Eve failed the bread test in the Garden of Eden when they ate the forbidden fruit (see Genesis 3:6).

The children of Israel failed the bread test when they didn't follow God's instructions and saved Manna for the next day. (See Exodus 16:20). And it is the same test many of us are failing today.

Hunger is one of the most powerful motivational forces on earth; it has caused people to steal and commit all kinds of other sinful acts to obtain food. The enemy knows this and seeks to use hunger to access our souls.

To pass the bread test, we should trust God to provide for all our needs. When we fully trust God, we will overcome the temptation to go after bread because we will instinctively rely on God's word instead of physical bread. By overcoming hunger and passing the bread test, Jesus demonstrated that he is the bread of life.

Faith Test

Jesus also had to pass the faith test in the wilderness. According to scripture, the devil took Jesus to the holy city, set Him on the pinnacle of the temple, and told Him, *"Throw Yourself down; angels will protect you."* While Jesus knew God gave His angels charge over Him, this was not the time to exercise that trust. Jesus told Satan, *"It is written again, 'You shall not tempt the Lord your God.'"* (Matthew 4:6-7). Jesus refused to obey the devil not because He did not believe that God gave angels instructions to protect him but because he refused to take orders from the devil. Jesus was completely submitted to God, which gave him the strength to resist the devil's temptation. Likewise, we should refuse to follow any directives from the devil.

Adam and Eve failed this same faith test in Genesis 3:1, when the serpent asked Eve, *"Did God really say, 'You must not eat from any tree in the garden?'"* The enemy will always try to get us to doubt what God says.

Israel failed the faith test in the wilderness when they doubted that God was with them. They questioned, *"Is the LORD among us or not?"* (Exodus 17:7). And it is the same test we fail when we doubt God will do what He said He would. You should never allow the devil to cause you to doubt what God has already told you. *"God is not human, that he should lie, not a human being, that he should change his mind. Does He speak and then not act? Does he promise and not fulfill?"* (*Numbers 23:19*).

To pass the test of faith, we must believe in God and believe in His promises. We should remain faithful even when it makes no sense to the natural mind, for His ways are higher than our ways and His thoughts our thoughts.

Love Test

When the devil realized he couldn't convince Jesus to doubt God, he offered Him a bribe. He showed Jesus all the kingdoms of the world and told Him, If you worship me, I will give them all to you." I call this the love test because Jesus had to demonstrate that He loves God more than He loves Himself or the glory of the world. Besides, Satan does not own the kingdoms of this world. The kingdoms of this world rightly belong to Jesus but fell under Satan's control because of sin. Jesus had to endure severe punishment for the sins of the world to reclaim the kingdoms of the world from Satan's control. So Satan tried to tempt Jesus to spare himself the punishment in exchange for bowing down and worshiping him. *Jesus said to him, "Then Jesus said to him, "Go away, Satan! For it is written, 'You shall worship the Lord your God, and serve Him only.' "* (Matthew 4:10).

Jesus remained faithful to God and chose to go through the process that The Father laid out for Him to obtain the kingdoms of the world. Jesus defeated Satan, took back all the kingdoms of the world that Satan tried to tempt Him with, and now He is the King of them all.

Eve failed in the Garden of Eden when she saw how desirable the tree was for gaining wisdom. She ate the fruit because she desired the knowledge it would give her (See Genesis 3:6). At that moment, her desire for knowledge became more than her desire for God. Israel also failed the love test in the wilderness when they worshiped the golden calf (See Exodus 32:5-6). Their desire for a tangible God overrides their desire for the Living God.

Although people don't physically worship a golden calf, their love for the things of this world has caused many people to fall into this trap. *"Do not love this world nor the things it offers you, for when you love the world, you do not have the love of the Father in you."* (1 John 2:15). Satan will often tempt us to give our worship to something that will make life easier for us, but in the end, it leads to an evil trap of sin. *"For the world offers only a craving for physical pleasure, a craving for everything we see, and pride in our achievements and possessions. These are not from the Father but are from this world. And this world is fading away, along with everything that people crave. But anyone who does what pleases God will live forever."* (1 John 2:16-17).

No matter how tough life becomes, we must love The Lord with all our hearts, souls, and minds (Matthew 22:37). When we love God with all our hearts and souls; we will not worship idols because God is the center of our lives.

Call to Action

Jesus emerged from the wilderness with great power after fasting for forty days and overcoming the devil's temptations. Having conquered his personal wilderness, he was now prepared and ready to take on the vast wilderness of sin.

Anyone God chooses to use for greater works will undergo a wilderness test of empowerment. So choose to conquer your wilderness and embrace the power of God. By the grace of God, you can pass the bread test, the faith test, and the love test. You already possess what it takes to overcome temptation, but you must apply it. Think of it this way: if the power goes out in your home and you have a generator hooked up, it will immediately kick in and power your home. Now that's how it is when you come to the end of yourself and have no fight left in you. The power generator of the Holy Spirit will activate and begin fighting for you.

So as you fast today, know that the tempter will come. He will try to oppose you in every way, but you are not alone. The Holy Spirit is with you. He strengthened Jesus to endure the temptation and will strengthen you too. Jesus overcame the devil's temptation even when He was at His weakest. Even when you are weak, God is strong in you. Don't rely on your own strength but on the strength of God.

Be aware that the enemy will tempt you to do things you would not normally do while fasting. He may even tempt you to complain against God for not answering your prayers quickly or tempt you to put God to the test. He might even tempt you to look for an easy way out of your wilderness, but trust God to give you spiritual strength to overcome your wilderness. Trust that God really does give His angel charge over you to keep you in all your ways.

PROMISE: *"For he will order his angels to protect you wherever you go. They will hold you up with their hands so you won't even hurt your foot on a stone."* (Psalms 91:11-12)

26

The Ultimate Fast

"When the time came, Jesus and the apostles sat down together at the table. Jesus said, 'I have been very eager to eat this Passover meal with you before my suffering begins. For I tell you now that I won't eat this meal again until its meaning is fulfilled in the Kingdom of God.' Then he took a cup of wine and thanked God for it. Then he said, 'Take this and share it among yourselves. For I will not drink wine again until the Kingdom of God has come." (Luke 22:14-18).

Did you know Jesus was fasting during the crucifixion? After He ate Passover with His disciples, He did not eat again. He told them that this would be the last time He ate and drank with them in this life. How often do we read over that scripture, not realizing that Jesus was fasting during the whole crucifixion? He fasted throughout the time He was arrested, sentenced, beaten, and crucified, which is an incredible feat to accomplish without any sustenance. I called this the ultimate fast because Jesus denied himself both physically and spiritually in every way possible. Let's take a deep dive into Jesus' ultimate fast to comprehend the depth of His passionate love for us. We will first examine His self-denial on the physical level, then on the spiritual level.

Physical Self Denial

Immediately after the last supper, Jesus and His disciples went to the Mount of Olives to pray. They later arrested Him there and sent Him to the home of Caiaphas, the high priest who questioned Him and sent Him to Pilate's Hall for trial. The Roman soldiers whipped him and handed Him back to the Jews to be crucified. Then He had to carry the cross on His back for eighty-two miles, then up the hill to Calvary while fasting.

Jesus didn't have time to eat or drink, nor was any food or drink offered to him while enduring the excruciating punishment for our sins. This was indeed the ultimate fast because Jesus denied himself everything; earthly possessions, sleep, clothes, food, drink, power, glory, love, and ultimately, His life.

Possessions

Many of us work hard to earn a living and achieve financial success, and many of us reach the peak of worldly success. But just think for a moment all the things we are striving for in this world cannot be compared to what Jesus gave up to rescue us from sin.

Jesus had it all, but He gave it all up because He loves us more than His glory. *"For you know the grace of our Lord Jesus Christ, that though He was rich, yet for our sakes, He became poor, so that you through His poverty might become rich"* (2 Corinthians 8:9). How many of us can give up what we own so that others might obtain the true riches of heaven? Jesus fasted from all worldly possessions to give us eternal riches.

Once, when a teacher of the law tried to follow Him, Jesus told him, *"Foxes have dens and birds have nests, but the Son of Man has no place to lay his head."* (Luke 9:58). Although everything was created by Him and for Him, He denied Himself everything. Not only did he give up

His heavenly possessions to come to Earth, but while living on Earth, he denied himself all earthly possessions so that we could share in His eternal ownership.

Sleep

Another thing that Jesus fasted during this ultimate fast was sleep. He did not sleep on the night of His passion; He spent the entire night praying in the garden of Gethsemane. According to Matthew 26:40-46, Jesus walked back and forth restlessly in the garden of prayer; his soul was in so much agony that He could not even think about sleeping. So he kept praying, *"My Father, if possible, may this cup be taken from me. Yet not as I will, but as you will."* Then he returned to his disciples and found them sleeping. He asked them, *"Couldn't you men keep watch with me for one hour?"*

In Matthew 26:39-41, Jesus told them to *"Watch and pray so that you will not fall into temptation. The spirit is willing, but the flesh is weak."* Although He wanted to sleep, His desire to do the Father's will was greater.

Jesus denied himself sleep and devoted Himself to praying to the Father for grace to endure the anguish He was about to experience. Although He denied Himself physical sleep after his passion on the cross, He entered the glorious rest of the Father.

Clothes

Jesus even fasted His clothing as he hung naked on the cross. According to Matthew 27:28-31,35, *"They stripped him and put a scarlet robe on him, and then twisted together a crown of thorns and set it on his head. They put a staff in his right hand. Then they knelt in front of him and mocked him. "Hail, King of the Jews!" they said. They spit on him, took the staff, and repeatedly struck him on the head. After they had mocked him, they took off the robe and put his own clothes on him. Then they led him away to crucify him." When they had crucified him, they divided up his clothes by casting lots.*

Jesus, being stripped of His clothes, goes way back to the Garden of Eden. After Adam and Eve sinned, they became ashamed of their nakedness, but God covered them in animal skin (Genesis 3:21). This shame of nakedness never left humanity and needed to be dealt with on the cross. Just like the innocent animal had to die and give up its innocent skin to cover Adam and Eve's nakedness, so too innocent Jesus was killed and stripped of his physical and spiritual clothes to cover the sins of humanity. Although Jesus did not sin, He had to bear the shame of sin as Adam and Eve did. So His nakedness on the cross dealt with the shame of sin once and for all.

After that terrible ordeal, Jesus never needed those clothes anymore because He is now robed in majesty, power, and great glory. Jesus gave his apostles a glimpse of what He would wear after His resurrection on the Mount of Transfiguration. Mark 9:3 say,s *"His clothes became shining, exceedingly white, like snow, such as no launderer on earth can whiten them."* He was clothed in the glistening glory of God. Apostle John later saw Him wearing a robe with a gold sash across his chest. (See Revelation 1:13). In another of His appearance to Apostle John, He was dressed in a robe dipped in blood, Revelation 19:13. Although he was stripped of His earthly clothes, Jesus is now fully robed in majesty, power, and great glory. And he promised a robe of righteousness to all those who love and serve Him. So Jesus gave up his clothes so that we could be clothed in His robe of His righteousness.

I Thirst

Then, as he hung naked, bleeding and dying on the cross, the one last thing he needed was a cup of cold water. Jesus did not eat or drink anything in the previous twenty-four hours of his scourging. He had lost a lot of bodily fluids through blood, sweat, and tears. So when He said, *"I thirst,"* He was extremely thirsty. Though some say, it was figurative thirst, but it was His body's physical need for water. The body can endure long periods without eating, but the body needs fluids to function, especially during strenuous, stressful situations like crucifixion. So Jesus was physically thirsty when He said, *"I thirst."* And they only offered him a bitter cup of wine mixed with gall.

It overwhelmed me to tears when I realized that humanity did not give a cup of cold water to the One who came to give us living water; we truly do not deserve it. According to John 7:37-38, *"On the last day, the climax of the festival, Jesus stood and shouted to the crowds, "Anyone who is thirsty may come to me! Anyone who believes in me may come and drink! For the Scriptures declare, 'Rivers of living water will flow from his heart.'"* So Jesus died on the cross to offer us living water, yet we refused to give him a cup of cold water. Just let that sink into your soul for a moment. We will not really know the extent of what Jesus did for us until we walk and talk with Him in glory. Therefore, Jesus fasted water so that we could receive His living water.

Spiritual Self-denial

In addition to denying himself physical things, Jesus also denied himself spiritually. Jesus denied himself power, love, and glory with the Father in order to enter the domain of sin and darkness because He had to take sin upon himself to pay its full penalty. Sin completely separated us from God, so Jesus had to become completely cut off from God to become our ultimate sacrifice. Jesus denied himself everything that sin denied us in order to save us. By nature, He was the most powerful man that ever walked the face of the earth, but He resisted using his power to defend himself as he went to the cross.

Power

Most people in a position of power would have used all the power at their disposal to save themselves from the painful humiliation that Jesus went through. Jesus had the power to call legions of angels and destroy the sinful world, but he denied Himself the use of that power. (see Matthew 26:53). Jesus chose to walk the painful path of humility so that He could fulfill the righteous requirements of the Father for our salvation. (see Matthew 26:54).

Instead of saving Himself, He saved us by fasting from the power that could have saved Him. The Lord Jesus fasted His power so that He could give us power over the enemy. He told us in Acts 1:8, *"But you will receive power when the Holy Spirit comes on you, and you will be my witnesses in Jerusalem, Judea, and Samaria, and to the ends of the earth."* We could not receive the power of the Holy Spirit until Jesus laid down His power. We were dead in our sins, but through faith in Jesus, God forgave our sins thus enabling us to be baptized with the power of the Holy Spirit.

Glory

Jesus fasted the glory that He had with His Father before the foundations of the world. There was nothing glorious about dying naked on a wooden cross. When He took the sins of the world upon himself, he was utterly cut off from the Father's glory. That is why he cried out, *"Father, why have you forsaken me?"* (Mark 15:34). At that moment, He was completely stripped of His glorious union with the Father. He felt forsaken because the sins of the world completely separate Him from the glory of the Father.

After His resurrection, Jesus prayed, *"Now, Father, bring me into the glory we shared before the world began."* (John 17:5). Jesus also prayed, *"I have given them the glory you gave me, so they may be one as we are one."* (John 17:22).

It is important to understand that if Jesus didn't give up his power and glory, they could not crucify him, and if they did not crucify Him, there would be no forgiveness of sins, and we could not share in his glory. Jesus fasted His glory so that he could bring us back to the glory of the Father.

Love Fast

As Jesus hung on the cross, he was devoid of love; He was fulfilling Isaiah's prophecy. *"He was despised and rejected as a man of sorrows, acquainted with the deepest grief. We turned our backs on Him and looked the other way. He was despised, and we did not care. Yet it was our weaknesses he carried; it was our sorrows that weighed him down. And we thought his troubles were a punishment from God for his own sins!"* (Isaiah 53:3). We were so depraved that we rejected the embodiment of love itself. Jesus was fasting for people who didn't know Him, including those who rejected and crucified Him. Remember, He prayed, *"Father, forgive them, for they do not know what they have done."* (Luke 23: 34). He was praying for the people who rejected Him, and He was praying for you and me.

Some of us know exactly what it feels like when no one loves you, but to have known the incomprehensible love of God and to be completely cut off from it is unimaginable. We can say that God loves us even if someone rejects us, but what if God himself rejects us? After Adam and Eve sinned, God rejected them and drove them out of the garden of Eden, and angels guarded its entrance with flaming swords (Genesis 3:24). To reunite humanity with God, Jesus had to be utterly cut off from the Father's love as we were because that is the penalty for sin.

The Lord Jesus could not fully take our sins upon himself until He was separated from the Holiness of God the Father. Therefore, He fasted the love of the Father to become a despised and rejected person. As painful as the physical cross was to bear, the rejection of the Father was the most incredible pain Jesus had to endure to bring us back into the love of the Father. There truly is no greater love than this.

His Life

The last thing that Jesus fasted for us was His life. In John 10:18, Jesus said, *"No man takes my life; I choose to lay it down for my friends."* He chose to deny himself the breath of life because the punishment of sin demands death, but this was no ordinary death because only a sinless sacrifice could fulfill the penalty of sin. (see Romans 6:23). No one on earth was righteous enough to pay that high price of sin until Jesus came. He was and still is the only Lamb of God who is worthy to take away the sins of the world.

We were spiritually dead in our sins and could not get back into the glorious, abundant life with God. Jesus loves us so much that he denied Himself to the point of death so that He could purchase eternal life for us with his sinless blood. In John 10: 28-30, He said, *"I give them eternal life, and they shall never perish; no one will snatch them out of my hand. My Father, who has given them to me, is greater than all; no one can snatch them out of my Father's hand. The Father and I are one."*

So the good news is when Jesus was raised to life by the power of the Holy Spirit, we who believe in Him are also raised to eternal life in Him. So through Jesus' death and resurrection, He denied Himself eternal life so that He could bring us back to the abundant, eternal, glorious life in God the Father.

Prophetic Foreshadowing

The incredible thing about this ultimate fast was that it was a prophetic foreshadowing of things to come and prophetic fulfillment of what was already prophesied about Jesus. All aspects of Jesus' life are a fulfillment of prophecy. In His ultimate self-denial, he became the Lamb of God that takes away the sins of the world. He becomes the King of Kings and Lord of Lords in His resurrection. Jesus became poor and destitute in every way possible to bring us to His eternal, glorious Kingdom.

The key to this ultimate fast was Jesus' complete obedience to God. Philippians 2:8 says, *"And being found in appearance as a man, he humbled himself by becoming obedient to death on a cross!"* He fasted physical and spiritual things to ensure we would become as rich in eternal things as He is. The Lord Jesus denied Himself earthly possessions, sleep, food, dignity, clothes, power, glory, and ultimately, His life. Nobody has ever denied themselves as completely as Jesus did, which is why He is the only way to heaven. No one can get to the Father without first believing and accepting His gracious payment for our sins. A fast like that has never happened before, nor will it ever happen again. That was the ultimate act of self-denial in every way possible. Jesus' ultimate fast was to please His Father and bring salvation to the world. His fasting and complete self-denial created an eternal gateway out of sin for us.

Jesus's rewards for this great fast were astounding. Jesus gained possessions of everything in heaven and earth. Revelation 5:12 says heaven worshiped him, *"Worthy is the Lamb that was slaughtered to receive power, wealth, wisdom, might, honor, glory, and blessing."* Jesus was rewarded with great power and glory for this ultimate fast. Oh, to see Him now in all his splendor and majesty!

Call to Action

So, as you fast today, focus on the eternal rewards rather than the earthly rewards. Be like Jesus; fast the temporary pleasures of this world so that you can possess eternal pleasures. Remember, it's not always about you and what you want to accomplish, but what God wants to do through us on the earth. Become obedient to the point of death, and do not allow anything to come between you and the

Savior's love.

When you face setbacks, failures, pain, or trauma in your life, keep your eyes focused on Jesus's sacrifice. Do not allow the pain of today to abort your future glory in the Lord. Understand that your pain is birthing you into a new dimension of Glory.

There is a glorious move of God coming to the earth, and He is looking for people who will selflessly deny themselves to fast and pray. When we fast to accomplish the will of God and not our own, we successfully touch the heart of God, and revival will come to the earth.

PROMISE: *"For in just a little while, the Coming One will come and not delay."* (Hebrews 10:37)

27

Apostles Fast

"Now in the church at Antioch, there were prophets and teachers: Barnabas, Simeon called Niger, Lucius of Cyrene, Manaen (who had been brought up with Herod, the tetrarch), and Saul." While they were worshiping the Lord and fasting, the Holy Spirit said, "Set apart for me Barnabas and Saul for the work to which I have called them." So after they had fasted and prayed, they placed their hands on them and sent them off." (Acts 13:1-3).

Despite the Lord's remarkable work at Antioch, the apostles began fasting. There is no indication of what prompted the fast. It does not appear that they were in any distress or received any prophetic word instructing them to fast. In fact, they were experiencing a revival. The gospel was being preached among the gentiles, and many people gave their hearts to the Lord. They were not in mourning or repenting as was customary during a fast, instead they were praising and worshiping while fasting.

I call those kinds of fasts glory fast because they were not fasting for blessings and breakthroughs but simply to touch the heart of God. Moses and Jesus did it, and now the apostles are doing it. Most people think that fasting is only about satisfying our desires, but fasting at its core is a bending of the human will to conform to the will of God. It is about finding out what the Lord wants us to do and then making ourselves do it. Let's explore the Apostle's fast to discover why the Holy Spirit prompted them to fast and what it means to us today.

Set Apart

The first indication of why the apostles were fasting came when the Holy Spirit said, *"Set apart for me Barnabas and Saul for the work to which I have called them."* Although a great revival was underway in Antioch, the apostles wanted to know what they should do next. So they fasted, and the Lord revealed through the prophets that He wanted Saul and Barnabas to be set apart from the group to do a special work.

The term set apart means to be chosen or reserved for a specific purpose. This means that the thing or person could not be used for any other purpose. Throughout the Bible, the Lord sets people apart for specific purposes. In Psalms 4:3, David said, *"Know that the Lord has set apart his faithful servant for himself; the Lord hears when I call to him."* David could state this so confidently because he remembered how he became king.

While David was tending his father's sheep on the backside of the desert, all of his brothers passed under Samuel's horn of the oil, but it did not pour down on them. The Lord rejected all of David's brothers, so his father called him in from the fields. Samuel immediately anointed David to be king over Israel, but he spent many years in the wilderness running for his life. (1 Samuel 16). David became the greatest king of Israel. David was confident that God set him apart for a specific purpose. Although he had to endure many trials, he embraced the call and believed he would be king one day. The Lord did the same thing many years later with Saul and Barnabas when He set them apart for a special work of preaching the gospel to the Gentiles.

A Special Work

The Lord revealed He wanted Saul and Barnabas to do a special work. It turns out that the special work was to spread the gospel in regions that had not heard it before. In those regions, the people either worshiped idols or were very religious, which made the gospel unwelcome. So, it was no simple task to travel and share the gospel because the persecution of Christians was rampant. Stephen and James were already martyred, and the believers were scattered in various regions. The scattered believers began preaching to the Gentiles, and revival broke out in Antioch.

The church at Jerusalem heard about the revival and sent Barnabas to check out the revival. He was so amazed by what he experienced that he went to Tarsus to look for Saul and bring him back to Antioch to minister to the Gentiles. He knew that Saul was the Lord's *chosen instrument to take His message to the Gentiles and kings, as well as to the people of Israel."* (Acts 9:15). Saul and Barnabas remained in Antioch for an entire year, preaching the gospel, building the church, and equipping the saints. During this time, the church at Antioch was thriving, so they fasted and prayed for the Lord's guidance on what they were to do next. Then Lord revealed His special work to them.

Preaching the gospel in hostile environments takes an extra measure of grace. Imagine being called to preach the gospel in Muslim, Buddhist, or communist countries such as Iran, China, or Russia. Despite your best efforts, they will not welcome you with open arms unless God's grace is with you. Yet missionaries today are called to do the same work as Paul and Barnabas. Some people are called to go into the darkest recesses of the earth to bring the light of God to the captives. The worse part of it is that the same people you are trying to reach are the same ones that could kill you. I read a story of a young missionary named John Allen Chau, who was killed by a remote Indian tribe because he tried to share the gospel with them. And there are many more like him who was killed in the line of duty of spreading the gospel. So there are real dangers when called to go into foreign territories to share the gospel.

Despite the hostile missionary environments, the apostles experienced many signs and miracles along the way. The sick were healed, the lame walked, and many people were converted. The missionary journey culminated in the establishment of numerous churches. Despite this remarkable move of God, there were many oppositions to the gospel. One man became mute because of opposing the gospel. Jewish leaders threw the apostles out of their synagogues and conspired to kill them. Apostle Paul was stoned and left for dead but got up and preached the gospel. Little did those hostile people know that when you are set apart for a particular purpose, you cannot die until it is fulfilled. This is why it is so important to find and pursue your calling. When you are pursuing your calling there is a special grace on your life, I like to say it like this, there is preservation in your purpose.

Strong Faith

It is easy to say 'yes' to God, but it is not always easy to do the will of God. Every person who answers the call of God faces many challenges, but the faithful ones endure to the end. Even when it becomes difficult, the Lord knows who will be faithful to His work. God knows how much we can handle, and He will not put more on us than we can take. Some mission requires people with strong faith and being filled with the Holy Spirit. Saul and Barnabas were chosen for this special work because of their strong faith and being filled with the Holy Spirit. I believe it is impossible to do the work of the Lord without the Holy Spirit and strong faith.

The Lord knew the task was difficult and would require strong faith and the anointing of the Holy Spirit. Therefore, Saul and Barnabas were well suited for this special work because they were full of faith and anointed by the Holy Spirit. *"Barnabas was a good man, full of the Holy Spirit and strong in faith."* (Acts 11:24). And Saul's Damascus Road experience left him blind for three days, during which he received tremendous revelations that transformed Him into a follower of Christ. Ananias laid his hand on Saul, and he received the Holy Spirit. (See Acts 9). To be chosen by God for a difficult task requires being filled with the Holy Spirit.

When working for the Lord, you must have complete faith in Him or you will quit and give up when trials come. Do you have the faith to endure persecution, to persevere against trials and tribulations? Without faith, it is impossible to embrace the demands of ministry. Do you know what you are anointed to do? Do you have enough faith to embrace your call?

Embracing the Call

It is important to understand your calling, and not try to operate in someone else's calling. The other three men who remained at Antioch had a different calling from Saul and Barnabas, but theirs was no less important. They were to remain in Antioch and continue the work while Saul and Barnabas went on their missionary journey.

When the prophet told me God called me to preach, teach, prophesy, and cast out demons, at first, I didn't embrace the call. It seemed too much for a young college kid. After much praying, fasting, and preparation, I eventually answered the call. It has been an adventurous ride filled with lots of hills and valleys, but through it all, God has never left my side.

Many times I wanted to give up, and I actually tried giving up the call, but that didn't work out well. The Lord told me you are a Jonah running away from your calling. Since I have no interest in the belly of a whale, the very next day, I committed to being faithful to the call no matter what it cost me.

Interestingly, both Saul and Barnabas fasted a second time, and the other apostles lay hands on them before they went on their missionary journey. The first fast reveals the call, but the second fast gave them the grace to execute the calling. Although we are filled with the Holy Spirit and have strong faith, it is commendable that you fast and pray before undertaking any great work for the Lord. The fact that they fasted a second time and the other leaders laid hands on them and prayed for them indicated they understood the magnitude of what they were about to face. Apostle Paul later gives us a glimpse of what he had to endure to answer the call of God. He said;

> *"I have worked harder, been put in prison more often, been whipped times without number, and faced death again and again. Five different times, the Jewish leaders gave me thirty-nine lashes. Three times I was beaten with rods. Once I was stoned. Three times I was shipwrecked. Once I spent a whole night and a day adrift at sea. I have traveled on many long journeys. I have faced danger from rivers and from robbers. I have faced danger from my own people, the Jews, as well as from the Gentiles. I have faced danger in the cities, in the deserts, and on the seas. And I have faced danger from men who claim to be believers but are not. I have worked hard and long, enduring many sleepless nights. I have been hungry and thirsty and have often gone without food. I have shivered in the cold without enough clothing to keep me warm. (2 Corinthians 11: 23-27)*

Amidst all that, Apostle Paul embraces his calling. Romans 1:1 says, "Paul, a servant of Christ Jesus, called to be an apostle and set apart for the gospel of God." He knew that although the task was difficult, he was the Lord's chosen instrument to take His message to the Gentiles.

196

(see Acts 9:15). He knew he was set apart for this difficult circumstance, so he gave himself fully to the work of The Lord. At one point, he also said, *"I have been crucified with Christ and I no longer live, but Christ lives in me. The life I now live in the body, I live by faith in the Son of God, who loved me and gave himself for me. (Galatians 2:20).* The only way to endure such a treacherous call was to have no fear of dying. The apostle's only concern was to fulfill his calling.

Call to Action

God is still setting people apart to do His great missionary work, but we must choose to accept the call. Matthew 22:14 says, *"For many are called, but few are chosen."* I have always wondered why only a few are chosen until the Lord whispered to me, *"The ones who accept the call are the ones who are chosen."* God is calling many people to the harvest, but few are choosing to accept the call. It's harvest time and the Lord needs all hands on deck because the harvest is plentiful, but the workers are few, and time is running out. (See Luke 10:2). He is looking for people who will accept the call and set themselves apart to work in His harvest.

Fasting and prayer demonstrate mastery over the flesh and enable you to be in the chosen few that labor in His harvest. Saul and Barnabas embraced their call through fasting and prayer. Embracing your call will take you through many trials and opposition. Therefore, it is important to fast and pray as you commit to the call.

If you are at a crossroads in your life or ministry or you feel like there is something more. That is a good time to fast and pray and ask the Lord what's next. Challenge the Lord for more, and he will reveal His plans to you. He will give you divine directions as you fast and seek his will.

So as you fast and pray today, ask the Lord of the Harvest to send laborers into the harvest. (Luke 10:2). Recognize and embrace the call that God has placed on your life. Prepare yourself to answer His call through fasting and prayer. Be willing to do whatever it takes to answer the call.

PROMISE: *"And I will show wonders in the heavens and in the earth: Blood and fire and pillars of smoke.* (Joel 2:30).

28

Bridegroom Fast

"Once when John's disciples and the Pharisees were fasting, some people came to Jesus and asked, "Why don't your disciples fast like John's disciples and the Pharisees do?" Jesus replied, "Do wedding guests fast while celebrating with the groom? Of course not. They can't fast while the groom is with them. But someday the groom will be taken away from them, and then they will fast." (Mark 2:18-20)

To understand what Jesus meant when he prophesied the days would come when the bridegroom would be taken away, and then the guest would fast, we will explore the three stages of the traditional Jewish wedding feast, which are engagement, preparation, and marriage feast. It is important to understand how this wedding feast applies to Jesus and the church as the bride of Christ. We must also understand what stage we are in prophetically speaking and how to prepare so that we are not left behind when He returns.

The Engagement

In the first stage of the marriage feast, the engagement or betrothal stage, the groom asks for the bride's hand in marriage. The parents of the bride sign a marriage covenant with the groom, and the groom pays a dowry to the bride's father. The groom is offered a cup of wine; he must sip from the cup and then offer it to his bride. The bride must also sip from the cup, expressing her willingness to marry the groom. They agree not to drink wine again until they drink it together on their wedding day.

The groom then puts a veil over the bride, which indicates that she is betrothed to him. The groom returns home to his father's house to prepare a place to receive his bride. The bride begins her own bridal preparation, which can last up to a year. Sometimes, they don't see each other again until their wedding day.

Once all the preparations were completed, it was customary for the bridegroom to return to claim his bride at midnight. The groom would blow a trumpet to notify the bride that he was coming. Once the trumpet sounded, she would quickly adorn herself and go out to meet her groom. A loud, festive, celebratory procession would lead back to the groom's house, where the wedding feast would begin. This wedding feast usually lasts for several days.

On their wedding day, both the bride and the groom fast from sun up until their first meal together as a married couple. They fast to purify themselves from previous sins so that they can begin their marriage in purity.

Jesus our Bridegroom

Jesus Christ first came to earth to sign the marriage contract or to enter a marriage covenant with us. He paid the dowry with His blood, and our Heavenly Father accepted and consented to this marriage. Revelation 5:9 says, *"You are worthy to take the scroll and to open its seals because you were slain, and with your blood, you purchased for God persons from every tribe and language and people and nation."*

Like the traditional Jewish bridegroom, Jesus also drank from a cup of wine and then offered it to his bride. Matthew 26:27-29 tells us that Jesus *"Took the cup, and gave thanks, and gave it to them, saying, "Drink from it, all of you. For this is My blood of the new covenant, which is shed for many for the remission of sins. But I say to you, I will not drink of this fruit of the vine from now on until that day when I drink it new with you in My Father's kingdom."*

So, Jesus offered his bride the same cup that he had to drink from. This cup represents two things, the cup of his death and suffering and the power of his resurrected life.

The cup of suffering consists of taking up our cross and following Jesus through death and suffering. The cup of His resurrection is eternal life, the new Jerusalem which we will drink from when we are glorified as He is. 2 Timothy 2:11-12 says, *"If we die with him, we will also live with him. If we endure hardship, we will reign with him. If we deny him, he will deny us."* So you see, we must be willing to drink from his cup to become His bride.

Although Jesus will never have to suffer as He did on Calvary, he will once more drink the cup of pain when He has to say to His sons and daughters who refused Him, *"Depart from me; I never knew you."* I imagine that will be even more painful than Calvary ever was because they will be lost for all eternity. But for those who are prepared to meet him, Jesus will sit and dine with them in the new Jerusalem. They will get to eat and drink the wine of the marriage supper with Jesus in glory.

The next thing that Jesus fulfilled in this wedding feast was the veil that the Jewish bridegroom gave his bride until his return. Jesus gave us the gift of the Holy Spirit, which signifies that we are engaged or betrothed to Him. 2 Corinthians 1:22 Says, *"He has identified us as his own by placing the Holy Spirit in our hearts as the first installment that guarantees everything he has promised us."* This is a sign to the world that we belong to Jesus and a constant reminder to us He is coming back to claim us as His own.

Similarly to the Jewish bridegroom, Jesus had to leave and prepare a place to receive his bride. In John 14:3, He told us clearly, *"And if I go and prepare a place for you, I will come back and take you to be with me that you also may be where I am."* So we patiently endure our trials as we await his return to claim us as His own. In the meantime, there is a lot of preparation to do before He returns.

Preparation

The traditional Jewish bride goes through her own personal preparation, both physically and spiritually. As part of the preparation, the bride would take special baths and apply scented oils and perfumes to her body. In preparation for meeting the king, Esther went through a whole year of beauty treatments, six months with oil of myrrh, and six months with perfumes and other beauty treatments for women. (see Esther 2:12). If Queen Esther had to prepare a whole year to marry an earthly king. How much more should we prepare and be ready to meet the King of Kings?

Our baptism in water and the Holy Spirit represents the special bath that prepares us to go before the King. Jesus said in John 3:5, *"Very truly I tell you, no one can enter the kingdom of God unless they are born of water and the Spirit."* Therefore, our baptism in water and the baptism in the Holy Spirit are essential preparations for Jesus' return.

Since the bride did not know the exact day or hour the groom would return, she would prepare her wedding garment, trim and oil her lamps, and wait for the sound of the groom's trumpet. Isaiah 61:10 gives us a glimpse of this wedding garment, *"I delight greatly in the LORD; my soul rejoices in my God. For he has clothed me with garments of salvation and arrayed me in a robe of righteousness, as a bridegroom adorns his head like a priest, and a bride adorns herself with her jewels."*

The traditional Jewish bride must also prepare herself mentally to give up everyone and everything she knows and dedicate herself to the groom. According to Genesis 24, Rebekah left everyone and everything she knew to become Isaac's wife in a foreign land. Likewise, we must be willing to give up everyone and everything to live with Jesus in his glorious homeland of heaven. Jesus said if we love our mother, father, or children more than we love Him, we are not worthy of Him. (See Matthew 10:37). So this bridegroom fast is to prepare for the return of Jesus Christ.

New Wineskin Fast

Jesus explained the 'bridegroom fast' this way; *"No one can put a new cloth on old cloth or new wine into old wineskins. The new patch would shrink and rip away from the old cloth, leaving an even bigger tear than before. The old wineskins would burst from the pressure, spilling the wine and ruining the wineskins. New wine is stored in new wineskins so that both are preserved."* (Matthew 9:16-17). Jesus explained that his disciples could not fast like John's disciples because their fasting was based on the old covenant of fasting for spiritual cleansing. (see Leviticus 23:27-28).

Fasting for atonement is no longer since Jesus' blood replaces the old wineskin fast of obtaining holiness through the law. His blood is now the only cleansing agent that can purify us from sin. There is nothing else for us to do but repent and accept it by grace through faith.

In Matthew 16:24, Jesus told his disciples, *"Whoever wants to be my disciple must deny themselves, (means to fast), and take up their cross and follow me."* The purpose of fasting must shift from fasting for spiritual cleansing to fasting to take up our cross. The new wineskin fast is not food fast, but a deep desire to be with Jesus. Our hearts should become so hungry for him that we give up everything to obtain Christ.

Lovesick for Jesus

The Shulamite woman best exemplifies this, longing for the Lord when she said, *I charge you, O daughters of Jerusalem. If you find my beloved, tell him I am lovesick!* (Song of Songs 5:8). When the friends of the Shulamite woman asked, what was it about her beloved that caused her to be so lovesick? She describes him like this.

*"My beloved is radiant and ruddy, outstanding among ten thousand. His head is purest gold; his hair is wavy and black as a raven. His eyes are like doves by the water streams, washed in milk, mounted like jewels. His cheeks are like beds of spice-yielding perfume. His lips are like lilies dripping with myrrh. His arms are rods of gold set with topaz. His body is like polished ivory decorated with lapis lazuli. His legs are pillars of marble set on bases of pure gold. His appearance is like Lebanon, the choice as its cedars. His mouth is sweetness itself; **he is altogether lovely my**. This is my beloved, friend, daughters of Jerusalem." (Song of Songs 5:10-16).*

In the same way that the Shulamite longed for her beloved's return, our souls should yearn for Jesus' return because he is our eternal lover of our souls. And if we were to describe the eternal lover of our souls, we would have to borrow the words of Apostle John in Revelation 1:14-16. He said, *"His head and his hair were white like wool, as white as snow. And his eyes were like flames of fire. His feet were like polished bronze refined in a furnace, and his voice thundered like mighty ocean waves. He held seven stars in his right hand, and a sharp two-edged sword came from his mouth. And his face was like the sun in all its brilliance."* That's our beloved people of God. He is altogether lovely!

When we think about Jesus, we often think of a Jewish man from Nazareth, but have you ever stopped to think about Him in

His glorified state? He is *altogether lovely,* too marvelous for our comprehension, and downright indescribable! There is something on the inside of us that just yearns to know Jesus. We must become so in love with Jesus that nothing else matters. That is what the new wineskin fast is about, a furious longing in our souls that can only be quenched when the trumpet sounds and Jesus returns to claim his bride, and we get to experience the depth of his marvelous love.

Sound of the Trumpet

Like the traditional Jewish bridegroom, Jesus will return to claim his bride, but no one knows the day of his return. 1 Thessalonians 4:16-17 gives us a little glimpse of what it will be like when He returns; it says, *"the Lord himself will come down from heaven with a commanding shout, with the voice of the archangel, and with the trumpet call of God. First, the believers who have died will rise from their graves. Then, together with them, we who are still alive and remain on the earth will be caught up in the clouds to meet the Lord in the air. Then we will be with the Lord forever."*

Sadly, some people will not be ready when that trumpet sounds, and it will be a great tragedy, for there will be weeping and gnashing of teeth. In the parable of the ten virgins, the five wise virgins were prepared, watching for the bridegroom to come, but the five foolish ones were unprepared. When the bridegroom came, the five wise virgins entered the marriage feast with the bridegroom, but the five foolish ones could not enter. (See Matthew 25:1-13). This is a prophetic forecast of what will happen when Jesus returns because many people are not preparing to meet the Savior when He returns. Therefore he told his disciples, *"You also must be ready all the time, for the Son of Man will come when least expected."* (Matthew 24:44). Although we do not know the hour or day of His return, we are certain that marriage supper will take place when Jesus returns.

Marriage Supper

The next stage of the traditional wedding feast is the marriage supper. The Feasts of Israel are an enactment of this great marriage supper between God and humanity. Israel has seven major feasts: Passover, Unleavened Bread, First Fruits, Feast of Weeks, or Pentecost. Jesus fulfilled four of the seven feasts of Israel, and He will fulfill the three remaining feasts when he returns: the Feast of Trumpets, the Day of Atonement, and the Feast of Tabernacle. The feast of trumpets is the seven trumpets explained in the book of Revelation. The Day of Atonement is when Jesus judges if we are worthy to enter the marriage supper, and the Feast of Tabernacle is when we tabernacle with him in the new Jerusalem. *"And I heard a loud voice from heaven saying, "Behold, the tabernacle of God is with men, and He will dwell with them, and they shall be His people. God Himself will be with them and be their God."* (Revelation 21:3). All of what we are going through now on the face of this earth is only preparation to Tabernacle with Jesus.

> *Then I heard what seemed to be the voice of a great multitude, like the roar of many waters and like the sound of mighty peals of thunder, crying out, "Hallelujah! For the Lord our God, the Almighty reigns. Let us rejoice and exult and give him the glory, for the marriage of the Lamb has come, and his Bride has made herself ready; it was granted her to clothe herself with fine linen, bright and pure, for the fine linen is the righteous deeds of the saints. And the angel said to me, "**Write this: Blessed are those who are invited to the marriage supper of the Lamb.**" And he said to me, "These are the true words of God."* (Revelation 19:6-9)

Only those who are prepared and ready to meet the bridegroom will enter the new Jerusalem. Revelation 21:27 says, *"Nothing evil will be allowed to enter, nor anyone who practices shameful idolatry and dishonesty—but only those whose names are written in the Lamb's Book of Life."* Therefore, it is so important to fast for the bridegroom and deny ourselves the pleasures of this present world so that we can reap the pleasures of eternal life. Nothing in this world can be compared to living in the glory of God.

Call to Action

So, as you fast today, do not fast using the old wineskin method of trying to cleanse yourself from sin, but fast with the understanding that Jesus' blood cleanses you from your sins. *"Jesus gave up his life to make us holy and clean, washed by the cleansing of God's Word. He did this to present us to himself as a glorious church without a spot or wrinkle or any other blemish so that at his coming, we will be holy and without fault."* (See Ephesians 5:25-27). Since Jesus already provided our cleansing, we need not fast for cleansing but fast instead to become one with him. All we need to do is deny ourselves, take up our cross, and follow Jesus into the ultimate fast of laying down our will to do His will.

The bridegroom fasting represents our willingness to forsake the pleasures of the world in order to live holy lives. Do not give in to temptations. Endure your trials patiently until the bridegroom returns, and give yourself fully to the work of the Lord.

Choose to live in the world but not of the world so that at Jesus's return, he will find you prepared and ready to enter the marriage supper without spot or wrinkle. Choose to live a fasted life.

Promise *"And if I go and prepare a place for you, I will come again and receive you to Myself; that where I am, there you may be also."* (John 14:3)

II

Benefits & Rewards of Fasting

This section of the book is focused on the health benefits and rewards of fasting.

Some of these rewards are found in Isaiah 58 and some in Joel 2; there are many other benefits and rewards that this study did not cover. Yet the topics covered as fasting rewards are sufficient to help you succeed in your fasting.

29

Health Benefits of Fasting

In recent years, research has shown that the practice of fasting yields tremendous health benefits. Fasting is like a natural detoxification of the body because it removes toxins and stimulates cells to produce enzymes that are normally repressed when the body intakes excess food. Although fasting does not cure diseases, it aids in the body's natural healing processes. Therefore, many people use fasting as a means to manage their weight and prevent disease. Although I will review some health benefits of fasting, it is important to note that I am not a medical doctor, and the information below should serve only as a reference. If you have any of the issues listed below, please seek medical help from a consulting physician.

Some of the many varied health benefits of fasting are cognitive health, weight loss, relief from chronic illness, digestive issues, blood sugar, and blood pressure control. Fasting may also aid with arthritis, muscular functions, and the reduction of cancer cells. We will discuss some of the most pertinent benefits on this list, but if you desire more information on the others, you can speak to your medical doctor or do a quick Google search. Medical Journals and science journals are the best sources to use for this kind of information. Let's discuss each benefit to understand how fasting affects our bodies.

Weight Loss

When you fast, you are limiting your calorie intake, which results in the body naturally breaking down stored fat cells to use for energy. When people are fasting for weight loss purposes, they do an intermittent fast whereby they limit themselves to eating set portions only at a certain time of day, almost like the Ezekiel Fast.

This type of fast is not about what you eat; it's about when you eat and how much you eat. The concept behind it is to give the body enough time to use up all the calories from the previous meal and tap into the body's stored energy before eating another meal.

Keep in mind that fasting for weight loss can be dangerous to your health if not done correctly. Some researchers have found that long periods without eating can encourage the body to store fat; therefore, if you are interested in fasting for weight loss, it should be done under a medical doctor's supervision.

There are specific ways to achieve and maintain weight loss goals during fasting, such as reducing the amount of food you eat and the times you eat it. There are varied schedules for intermittent fasting that can help you lose weight. I prefer the 16:8 schedule, which seems to be the most popular one. This involves eating only during an 8-hour window of the day and fasting for the next 16 hours. Some people prefer the 5:2 schedule, in which they fast for two specific days per week and eat normally for the other five days. You should choose what schedule works best for you.

Blood Pressure

High blood pressure is another common and deadly condition that is affecting millions of people today. Researchers have found that periodic fasting can help to reduce blood pressure. This happens because of two reasons.

First, the body is not receiving its normal diet, which may contain triggers such as sodium that could increase blood pressure. Second, the body's metabolic processes rest during fasting, which lowers the heart rate and decreases blood pressure.

Blood Sugar

When we fast, the body is forced to produce its own glucose from stored energy or fat cells. The body can naturally produce its own sugar, but when it is constantly fed excess sugar, instead of producing sugar, it stores sugar. When it does not receive the sugar and carbohydrates that it normally receives, it resorts to a process called ketosis, in which the liver breaks down stored fat to produce energy.

Another way that fasting lowers blood sugar is to lower insulin production in the body. When the body is constantly receiving sugar, it keeps creating insulin, but if there is too much insulin in the blood cells, it will stop producing insulin. This can cause the cell to become insulin resistant, resulting in high glucose content in the bloodstream. When this happens, some doctors are turning to intermittent fasting to reset the body's insulin production process.

If you are hypoglycemic, you should not attempt to use fasting for blood glucose control. People have reported fainting from lack of food for long periods of time. This happens because blood sugar levels drop too low. Again, you should discuss any concerns you have with your medical doctor.

High Cholesterol

The number of people taking cholesterol medication is increasing, and most of those medicines have major side effects. One side effect of leading cholesterol medication is said to cause a stroke. So some doctors are recommending intermittent fasting to reduce cholesterol.

The primary way that you can reduce cholesterol levels is to cause your body to burn fat. You can do so by eating fewer calories and by exercising. However, it is not recommended to do both at the same time. During fasting, your body needs rest to accommodate the dietary and metabolic changes taking place. When you fast, you naturally lower your calorie intake, forcing the body to burn fat and reduce cholesterol.

Digestion

Another great benefit of fasting is that it cleanses the digestive system. Over the years, when people eat food, residues get stuck in their intestines and can remain there for years.

Fasting results in an empty stomach, but the production of digestive juices continues for the first few days of fasting. When this happens, the stomach acids work on the walls of the stomach to remove the stuck food. Usually, when you get hungry, you can feel the production of stomach acid. The stomach acids will break down stuck food on the stomach walls of the intestines since there is no food for it to digest. It is recommended to drink water to help this cleansing process continue in your stomach.

Also, keep in mind that if this process is prolonged, it can lead to ulcers in the stomach. Fasting is not recommended for people who are having stomach issues. If you are having stomach problems, it's best to do a partial fast and progress to full fast as you can. Again, consult a medical doctor.

Cardiac Health

The leading contributors to heart disease are high blood pressure, obesity, diabetes, and high cholesterol. When you fast, all these risk factors are lowered naturally; fasting also aids in cardiac health. When your body is not absorbing food that it normally stores, it resorts to breaking down what is already stored, which results in resetting various processes of the body, including optimal functioning of the heart.

Most cardiac-related issues are associated with the diet we feed ourselves; therefore, if we periodically fast, it will help the body reset itself and cleanse the body from the build-up of toxins introduced by the food we eat. Keep in mind that the more weight your body has, the harder it is for the heart to pump blood, but as your weight decreases, there is less pressure on the heart to pump the blood around the body, thereby reducing the blood pressure and enhancing cardiac function.

Mental Focus

Have you ever noticed that you get drowsy or tired when you eat? That is because the blood rushes to the stomach organ to aid in the digestion process. When you are fasting, the digestion process is at rest, and the energy you would normally use to digest food is now available to be used by the brain.

Also, when you fast, there are fewer toxic residues flowing through your blood and lymphatic system. This means that the body has less cleaning up process to do, and more blood energy is now available to support brain functions, making it easier for you to think, focus and recall information. Be warned that the first few days of fasting are called detox days. You will experience food withdrawal symptoms such as headaches and fatigue, but these are temporary.

It is important to keep in mind that fasting is not a cure. It is a catalyst that jumpstarts various physiological processes in the body. It aids the body as it performs its natural metabolic processes more efficiently.

30

Isaiah's Rewards of Fasting

"Then your light will break forth like the dawn, and your healing will quickly appear; then your righteousness will go before you, and the glory of the LORD will be your rear guard" "Then you will call, and the LORD will answer; you will cry for help, and he will say: Here I am 'If you get rid of the yoke of oppression, the pointing of the finger and malicious talk, and if you spend yourselves on behalf of the hungry and satisfy the needs of the oppressed, then your light will rise in the darkness, and your night will become like the noonday." (Isaiah 58:8-10).

The many rewards and benefits of fasting are extensive. Fasting produces great health benefits and God rewards us for our efforts in fasting and prayer.

Some people have reported weight loss and other health benefits as a result of their fasting. Fasting is so beneficial to peoples health that it is used in some holistic medical field as cure for some illnesses.

Many people reported divine healing and breakthroughs after or during their fasting. However, the rich spiritual benefits of fasting far supersede any physical benefits that we could derive.

God promises over ten different rewards for fasting in Isaiah 58 if our fast is acceptable to Him; revelation, healing, righteousness, the glory of God, quick answers to prayers, continual guidance, refreshing, lasting work, and restoration. If you are like me, you want every one of these promises, so let's find out more about these fasting rewards.

Revelation

Fasting accelerates revelation. God told the people that if they fasted acceptably, their light would shine in the darkness. Light symbolizes revelation. Daniel fasted to receive revelation about the future of his nation, and an angel gave him the revelation he was praying for. (See Daniel 9:21-23). When you fast expect angelic visitations, sometimes you will see them, and other times you will just know they are there. I once saw a huge angel sitting on the roof over my bedroom; I wondered what he was doing there, but no revelation was given to me. Later on, I was praying about a tormenting spirit that was attacking me at night. I remember feeling like the Lord was not helping me because I would go through the same thing night after night. At some point in my complaint to the Lord, He reminded me of the angel I saw earlier, and I then realized He sent the angel long before the demonic attack came. So you see, God already provided the angel to protect me even before the attack began. I needed the revelation to understand why the angel was there and that I was not in this battle by myself.

So you may or may not have angelic encounters when you fast, but you always have the Holy Spirit guiding you into the revelatory truths of God. John 16:13 says, when the Spirit of truth comes, he will guide you into all truth. He will not speak on his own but will tell you what he has heard. He will tell you about the future. God will reveal his plan to you when you fast, sometimes through visions, a prophetic word, or angelic visitation.

Healing

God wants to heal you through fasting, but you must meet his conditions. We cannot expect to reap the benefits of fasting unless we abide by God's principles. Remember, a man looks at the outward appearance, but God looks at the heart. He sees the unconfessed sins and impure motives of our hearts. Remember that in Matthew 15:26, Jesus said healing is the children's bread. So, by logical reasoning, it should be relatively easy for children of God to receive healing, but we know it has not been easy for some people to receive healing. So two questions came to mind; Who are God's children, and how do they eat the bread of healing? To become a child of God, you must be born of the water and the Spirit. *"For all who are led by the Spirit of God are children of God. So you have not received a spirit that makes you a slave to fear. Instead, you received God's Spirit when he adopted you as his own children. Now we call him "Abba, Father."* For His Spirit joins with our spirit to affirm that we are God's children. (Romans 8:14-16). So we become children of God when we receive His Spirit, and His spirit lives in us.

Now, we must pull up a chair at the Lord's table and eat the bread of healing, but how do we do that? Jesus says if we have faith in God, we can ask for anything in his name, and we will receive it. (Mark 11:22-24 and John 14:13). To eat from the bread of healing, you must do two things; believe in your heart and pray. It is not enough to pray, and it is not enough to believe. If you pray, you must believe; if you believe, you must pray. Believe, pray, and you will receive your healing.

You may say, but I have been praying, and nothing is happening. Let's find out why; look at the next two verses in Mark 11:25-26, "But when you are praying, first forgive anyone you are holding a grudge against so that your Father in heaven will forgive your sins." "But if you do not forgive, neither will your Father in heaven forgive your trespasses." Unforgiveness is the number one barrier to eating the bread of healing.

There may be other barriers to receiving your healing, but when you come to the Lord's table, you first need to check your heart before you can eat the bread of healing. This makes fasting so important because it's like a heart check. Anytime you genuinely fast and pray, God will reveal hidden things in your heart and help correct them so that you can eat from the bread of healing. We cannot expect healing or answers to prayers if there are unconfessed sins in our hearts. We will only be able to experience this healing or breakthrough when we align our hearts with the heart of God by obedience. The Holy Spirit will help us see our faults and give us the grace to repent; then our healing will come quickly.

Glory

When you fast to seek God's heart, the glory of the Lord will fill your heart and soul. Isaiah puts it this way: the glory of the LORD will be your rear guard. The glory of God protects your life. Just think about Moses leading the children of Israel through the wilderness; the pillar of cloud in the day and the pillar of fire at night was God's glory manifesting among his people. When you are in the manifested glory of God, He will go before you and fight on your behalf, just as He did for the Israelites. (Deuteronomy 1:30). We often walk in God's glory but don't recognize it. We expect the glory to manifest spectacularly like a pillar of cloud or fire; when it doesn't, we are disappointed. We need to learn how to recognize the glory of God in our everyday lives.

There are three primary ways that the glory of God is expressed in our lives; We can feel, hear, and see the glory of God. To help you recognize the glory, let's consider the three words in the Bible that represent glory. The first word is Kavod, which means weight or worth. The second is Shekinah, which means God's divine presence. The third is Doxa, which means splendor. These words have various meanings that we don't have room to discuss here. Our focus here is to provide enough information so that you recognize the glory of God in your own life.

Let's look at some examples of each representation of the glory. An example of the Kavod is found in 1 Kings 8:11-12, "And when the priests came out of the Holy Place, a cloud filled the house of the LORD, so that the priests could not stand to minister because of the cloud, for the glory of the LORD filled the house of the LORD. The glory of God can feel like a weight but a good, sweet weight. Because of the weight of the glory, the priest could not stand. Have you ever felt the presence of God so strongly that you could not stand? If so, you have been in the glory of God.

An example of the Shekinah is found in Exodus 16:10, "The glory of the LORD dwelt on Mount Sinai, and the cloud covered it six days. And on the seventh day, he called to Moses out of the midst of the cloud." The divine presence of God can manifest in many ways; people speak of angelic encounters, gold dust appearance, and cloud-like conditions inside a closed building or on top of the building. To the natural eyes, it looks like just a cloudy day or a mist of some sort, but could those things be a manifestation of God's glory? Could it be God making his presence known to us?

An example of the Doxa is found in Luke 2:9. And an angel of the Lord appeared to them, and the glory of the Lord shone around them, and they were filled with great fear. I called this the glistening glory because it's like a bright, sparkling cloud of light that is alive. But Doxa is not just glistening light; it also represents the Word became flesh and dwelt among us, and we have seen his glory, glory as of the only Son from the Father, full of grace and truth. (John 1:14). So you see, you can find glory in the seemingly mundane things in life; after all, the Bible says, the whole earth is filled with the glory of the Lord.

There are many more expressions of God's glory in both the Old and New Testament, and it would take another book to discuss them all. However, you can use the above example to look for the glory of God in your life and in your Bible reading. God's heart grieves to see his children searching for His glory when He is right there with them. Think about this: what if the Israelites saw the burning mountain and said oh, that's just a wildfire; let's keep looking for the cloud, or if they saw the glory cloud and said, it's just a cloudy day; let's look for the fire. We don't recognize the glory of God in the manger; we don't recognize the glory of God in the manna and the quail; we don't recognize him in our everyday life because we keep looking for something else. How about we stop and behold the Shekinah glory that lives in us?

The glory of God in your life frees you from worrying about the future and empowers you to trust Him completely. When you are walking in God's glory, your path will grow brighter each day. Even though you face struggles, setbacks, and failures, they will not overcome you. If you want the glory of God in your life, you must fast by God's standards, not yours. His standards for fasting are to keep his commandments and give Him all your heart, and then His glory will be your rear guard as you fast.

Righteousness

Isaiah also said another benefit of fasting is that your righteousness will go before you. This means that your righteousness will lead you. People's reputations, whether good or bad, often precede them. Your righteousness will be the first thing people see or hear about. So what exactly is righteousness? Righteousness is to be justified by God. No one can make or declare themselves righteous; it is a gift of God that can only be received through faith. Romans 1:16-17 says, "For I am not ashamed of the gospel of Christ, for it is the power of God to salvation for everyone who believes, for the Jew first and for the Greek. For in it, the righteousness of God is revealed from faith to faith; as it is written, "The just shall live by faith." You get the gift of righteousness by faith, but you must pursue it.

If you are not hungry for righteousness, you will never pursue it. Matthew 5:6 says, Blessed are those who hunger and thirst for righteousness, for they shall be filled." If you hunger for God's righteousness, He will give it to you. Your desire for righteousness will cause you to pursue it. And by the way, righteousness is a person. His name is Jesus. When you pursue Jesus, you are pursuing righteousness because you cannot become righteous without Jesus. You must have faith in his redemptive work on the cross; that is the only way to receive His robe of righteousness.

You need the righteousness of God in your life and in your nation because there is provision, protection, and exaltation in righteousness. King David says, I have been young, and now I'm old, yet I have not seen the righteous forsaken. (Psalm 37:25). With all the uncertainties happening around us today affecting our health and prosperity, it is important to seek the righteousness of God because he will always provide for those who trust Him.

Not only does he provide for the righteous, but he protects them. Proverbs 13:6 says, *"Righteousness guards him whose way is blameless, but wickedness overthrows the sinner."* There is a distinction between people who practice righteousness and those who practice lawlessness and immorality. There is protection in righteousness; just think of the breastplate of righteousness in Ephesians 6:14. It guards and protects the vital organs, such as your heart. When righteousness guards your heart, the wellspring of life will flow from it.

Righteousness elevates people and nations. According to Proverbs 1 4:34, "Righteousness exalts a nation, but sin is a reproach to any people." Over the course of history, it is well documented that nations who revere God and practice righteousness prospered and excelled in their endeavors, while others who practice lawlessness struggled to survive. When your ways are pleasing to the Lord, He says your gift of righteousness will make room for you and bring you before great men. Fasting helps you to turn away from your sins and embrace the gift of God's righteousness by faith.

Answered Prayers

When we fast according to God's terms and conditions, He promises to answer and say, "Here I am." Isaiah 58:9 "If you do away with the yoke of oppression, with the pointing finger and malicious talk, and if you spend yourselves on behalf of the hungry and satisfy the needs of the oppressed, God will answer our prayers. Removing the yoke speaks of forgiveness; we must forgive others of their trespasses because, in Matthew 6:12, Jesus taught his disciples to " forgive us our debts, as we forgive our debtors." We cannot take people hostage; in our minds, if we want God to answer our prayers, we must forgive others for their offenses.

The next thing God wants us to do before he answers our prayers is to stop speaking negatively of each other. When we speak negatively about each other, it grieves the heart of God because He loves all of His children. We are all God's children, and He loves us all the same. When people offend us, we should always respond with love because 1 Peter 4:8 says, "Above all, love each other deeply, because love covers over a multitude of sins." When you love people, you will not be inclined to speak evil against them. Besides, Proverbs 18:21 tells us that the power of life and death is in the tongue. We should therefore choose to speak life instead of death.

Let us choose to use our tongues to speak life instead of vicious rumors. It is so easy to fall into gossip and backbiting if we are not careful in our communication. Many of us are careful to do the big things while the little foxes are spoiling the vines. Most Christians do not act immorally or commit obvious sins, but the words we think and speak may prevent us from receiving answers to our prayers. Examine what you think and speak about others to ensure no iniquity is in your heart. Even if people hurt you, think positively and allow God to heal you from the pain they caused. Remember, Jesus is your comforter, not the person who hurt you. Go to the Lord Jesus and ask him to comfort you as you endure painful situations.

Well-watered Garden

God also told the people in Isaiah 58, "You shall be like a well-watered garden, whose waters will not fail" (Isaiah 58:11). God will cause you to thrive like a well-watered garden, even through the droughts of life. But there are conditions to be met if we are to become a well-watered garden. The preceding verse tells us to *"Feed the hungry, and help those in trouble. Then your light will shine out from the darkness, the surrounding darkness you will be as bright as noon."* (Isaiah 58:10). We must couple our giving with our fasting. Be kind to others, feed the hungry, and help people who are in trouble. Why is this so important to God? That's the best way to show the love of God. He wants people to know He loves them, and since we are his hands and feet, we must demonstrate his love to those in need.

Being watered by God represents peace and prosperity in your heart and soul. Elijah lived through a drought season, yet he did not experience any lack because God watered him like that well-watered garden. The drought sometimes reminds us to appreciate the rain, and the famine reminds us to appreciate the abundant seasons.

One way to experience being watered by the Lord during seasons of drought is to remain in the Vine. *"I am the true vine, and my Father is the gardener. He cuts off every branch in me that bears no fruit while every branch that does bear fruit he prunes so that it will be even more fruitful."* (John 15:1-2). Jesus is the vine that gives us access to the living waters, to the River of Life; as long as we abide in him, we will never thirst. To abide in him means we must keep believing and trusting in his goodness.

He said in John 15:16-17 says. *"You did not choose me, but I chose you and appointed you so that you might go and bear fruit—fruit that will last—and so that whatever you ask in my name, the Father will give you.* Think of many fruits on a tree branch, and each one placing a demand on the tree's sap to pull the nutrients from the ground. As long as those fruits remain on the branches, they will continue to receive nutrients, but once they are removed from the branch, they stop growing. If you want to reach your full potential in Christ, you must remain faithful to God. He is the gardener of our hearts and knows when and how to prune and water them. Fasting is God's pruning hook; it pulls up those dead, withered plants of pride and pains of your past and allows him to plant new ones. The pruning process will not be pleasant, but if you repent and allow God permission to prune your heart and life. He will root out rejection, fears, failure, bitterness, and everything hidden there and plant new seeds of love, gentleness, kindness, goodness, humility, grace, and mercy in the garden of your heart. Then, you will thrive like the well-watered garden you were intended to be.

Restoration

God also promised to restore and rebuild the broken-down places of your life when you fast according to His prescribed manner. Isaiah 58:12 says, *"Those from among you shall build the old waste places; You shall raise the foundations of many generations; and you shall be called the repairer of the breach, the restorer of streets to dwell in."* Fasting is a spiritual tool that rebuilds the foundation of holiness and righteousness. It restores the right relationship with God and repairs the broken-down edges where we compromise in our walk with the Lord.

God is complete, sufficient, and perfect in every way, and that is precisely what He wants for us. He wants to restore us to our pre-fallen condition, where we once walked in fellowship with Him. Psalm 12:1-2 puts it way, *"When the Lord restored the fortunes of Zion, we were like those who dreamed. Our mouths were filled with laughter, our tongues with songs of joy. Then it was said among the nations, "The Lord has done great things for them."* God wants to restore everything that the enemy stole from us; marriages, families, finances, health, and strength, but He cannot do so until we humble ourselves and keep his commandments.

God also promises to restore lost time. In Joel 2:25-27, The Lord says, *"I will restore to you the years that the swarming locust has eaten, the crawling locust, the consuming locust, and the chewing locust, My great army which I sent among you. You shall eat in plenty, be satisfied, and praise the name of the Lord your God, who has dealt wondrously with you, and My people shall never be put to shame. Then you shall know that I am in the midst of Israel: I am the Lord your God, and there is no other."* He allowed those years to be eaten up by the locust to help us see our faults, repent, and seek Him with all our hearts. When we return to God and allow Him to prune our lives, He will restore lost years, provision, satisfaction, rejoicing, and dignity.

Ride on Heights

In Isaiah 58:13, the Lord also promises, "If you keep your feet from breaking the Sabbath, he will cause you to ride on the heights of the land." Rest is the condition that needs to be met for you to ride on the heights of the land. It is essential to God, both spiritually and physically. Most of us do not have a problem resting physically, but we do not know how to rest spiritually. Spiritual rest includes choosing to rest from anxieties; worries, cares, concerns, fears, etc. Spiritual rest means that you place your cares on the Lord. 1 Peter 5:7 *Cast all your anxiety on Him because He cares for you.*

When we learn to rest in the goodness of God, it will cause us to trust, and he will make our feet like hind feet. Habakkuk 3:19 says,

"The Sovereign Lord is my strength; he makes my feet like the feet of a deer; he enables me to tread on the heights." In other words, God will cause you to walk places where others slip and fall. I have seen the little goats up on the cliff side that other animals cannot climb. When you are confident in the Lord's ability to elevate you and promote you, he will cause you to go places and do things you could only dream of doing.

Many people testify of receiving promotions and breakthroughs after or during their fast, and this is marvelous, but do not set your heart upon those things. Appreciate them for what they are, but seek to increase in the wisdom, knowledge, understanding, power, and glory of the Lord. God wants us to grow in wisdom and power because He wants to elevate us and use our gifts to promote us in power and authority.

31

Joel's Rewards of Fasting

"Then the LORD will be zealous for His land and pity His people.' The LORD will answer and say to His people, "Behold, I will send you grain, new wine, and oil, and they will satisfy you; I will no longer make you a reproach among the nations." (Joel 2:18-19)

The benefits and rewards of fasting do not end with those listed by Isaiah because Joel chapter two also promises tremendous blessings for the people who will humble themselves before God in true fasting and prayer. God promised to send new grain, wine, and oil and He also promised to deliver them from the northern army and pour out His Spirit upon them.

New Wine

The promise of new wine, oil, and grain was extremely important to the people in Joel's day because the land was bare and destitute due to famine and plagues of locust. The people depended on God for the produce of their fields but there was no rain and their crops failed and locust devoured it whatever was left. This happened because they were being punished for their sins of idolatry. Yet in their distress God in His great mercy promised new wine, grain and oil.

This is was a pledge of God's faithfulness to the people, although they sinned and He punished them, He wanted them to know that He was still merciful and would not totally abandon them. When God withheld the rain and the produce of the land, it was only to bring their attention to severity of their sins. Then he told them in 2 chronicles 7:14 if they fast, pray and return to him he would heal their land. So when Joel told the people that God would cause the rain to come come in abundance and their crops would yield bountiful harvest, he was reminding of God's promise. Amos 9:13 mirrors this promise as well, because it says, *"The days are coming," declares the Lord, "when the reaper will be overtaken by the plowman and the planter by the one treading grapes. New wine will drip from the mountains and flow from all the hills,"* Again we see the promised of new wine. Its important to understand that new wine is produced from the crushing of grapes, new oil from the crushing of olives, and new grain from the threshing of wheat. These process can seem destructive at first until the oil, wine or grain is extracted. This promise of new wine was twofold in that while God was giving them literal new wine, He was going to make a new nation out of them. So in essence God was telling the people that although they were going through a crushing or threshing process new wine would be produced out of their pain.

New wine is symbolic of three things, renewal, joy and the Holy Ghost. When you fast and pray and genuinely seek the heart of God. He will renew your mind and heart. He will fill you with a profound sense of joy and peace. And he will fill you with his Spirit which we will discuss later in this chapter.

Deliverance

The next thing God promised he would do for Israel's children was to remove the northern army. In Joel 2:2, He says, *"Then I will remove far from you the northern army and will drive him away into a barren and desolate land, with his face toward the eastern sea and his back toward the western sea; his stench will come up, and his foul odor will rise because he has done monstrous things."* For the children of Israel, there was a literal northern army oppressing them, but for us as believers today, when the Lord says He will drive away the Northern Army, it represents things that are oppressing us.

Oppression usually occurs when our lives are not in the correct alignment with the will of God and fasting helps us realign ourselves with God's purpose for our lives. To recognize oppression in your life you must understand what it means. By definition, oppression is a sense of being weighed down in body or mind. There are different kinds of oppression, but my focus here is on spiritual oppression. Keep in mind that oppression is different from depression. Oppression is external, while depression is internal. However, if oppression is left unchecked, it can lead to depression.

Oppression in a believer's life happens for three main reasons; generational curses, witchcraft, and rebellion. These kinds of oppression manifest through Chronic illnesses, poverty, failures and rejection.

If you find yourself going through multiple chronic illnesses simultaneously, you may be dealing with a spirit of oppression. When this happens most likely, there is an open door that is giving the enemy access to your health. Some open doors could be offense, unresolved trauma, fear, shame, doubt, and unforgiveness. Curses will have no effect on your life if there aren't any doors for them to operate through because as Proverbs 26:2 says a curse causeless shall not land. If there are no access points for the curse to penetrate your life it will not be effective against you.

Poverty and financial lack are other signs of oppression. Many people live paycheck to paycheck, barely making ends meet. Maybe you find that everything you earn is going through the back door. You labor and toil all day long, but is not able to enjoy the fruit of your labor. Chances are there is enemy access to your finances. Some access could be a generational curse of poverty or unwise financial decisions.

Emotional issues is another kind of oppression that plagues peoples lives. Sometimes people may find themselves caught up in emotional turmoil, going through bouts of, sadness, anger, and despair without any reasonable explanation; usually, there is a Devil loose.

Chronic failure is another kind of oppression that often plagues people's lives. If you find that you failed at everything you tried or you have no purpose or passion for life, you may be dealing with spiritual oppression. One clear indication of oppression is the failure to thrive in environments that are conducive to success. Despite our best efforts, sometimes we face periods of unsuccessfulness, lack of productivity or progress, and we do not know why. When this happens, unseen forces are working against us to cause barrenness and failure in our lives.

The good news is, fasting and praying with the right motives can remove these "Nothern Armies" from your life and cause us to become productive and successful again. When you fast, God promises to remove oppression from you. Isaiah 54:14 also says, *"In righteousness, you shall be established; you shall be far from oppression, for you shall not fear; and from terror, for it shall not come near you."* As powerful as oppression is, the Power of God is greater. You do not need to fear oppression because God has given you all you need to overcome oppression. 1 John 4: 4 says, *You, dear children, are from God and have overcome them because the one in you is greater than the one in the world.* The Holy Spirit, the spirit of Jesus, is living inside of you. And James 4:7 also says, *"Submit yourselves, then, to God. Resist the devil, and he will flee from you."* When you are operating under God's authority, you can victoriously resist the enemy and defeat oppression and depression.

Double Portion

Another wonderful reward of fasting is the double portion blessing. In Joel 2:23, *"Be glad, people of Zion, rejoice in the Lord your God, for he has given you the autumn rains because he is faithful. He sends you abundant **autumn** and **spring** showers, as before.* Observe that both autumn and spring rain came at the same time. God wanted the to people understand that they will receive a double for their troubles. As Isaiah 61:7 Says, *"Instead of your shame you will receive a double portion, and instead of disgrace you will rejoice in your inheritance. And so you will inherit a double portion in your land, and everlasting joy will be yours."* Observe that the double portion does not come until after a season of testing. God will allow those seasons of testing to cause us to see the error of our ways and repent from them. If we genuinely repent and return to God in fasting and prayer He will cause the dry places in our lives to spring back to life and yield double portions of blessings. In Joel 2:21-22, He said, *"Don't be afraid, O land. Be glad now and rejoice, for the Lord has done great things. Don't be afraid, you animals of the field, for the wilderness pastures will soon be green. The trees will again be filled with fruit; fig trees and grapevines will be loaded down once more."* To fully appreciate this promise keep in mind the living conditions of the people during Joel's time. The land was experiencing a season of drought because the people sinned against the Lord. The prophet told them that if they repented and returned to the Lord, He would restore their crops in abundance. The sign to the people that God would keep his promise was the abundant Spring and Fall rain.

When you fast, God will cause double portions of blessings to come to you, those that have been held back and those that are for this current season of your life. If you feel like your blessings are delayed, repent, pray, fast, and wait for the rain.

232

Overflow

A season of abundance often follows a period of sincere repentance. In Joel 2:24, The Lord also promised that the *"threshing floors will be filled with grain; the vats will overflow with new wine and oil."* but remember that both grain and grapes require time to grow. So, it may take a while to see the manifestations of your prayers. However, it can also happen suddenly when we meet God's conditions for overflow. It is not up to us when or how it happens, but we must trust and believe that God is faithful to do what he promised because He cannot lie.

Growing seeds and reaping a harvest require patience, but Galatians 6:9 *"Let us not become weary in doing good, for at the proper time we will reap a harvest if we do not give up."* Many people fast and expect the harvest to appear the next day, but you must understand that there is seed, time, and harvest. Think of it this way a farmer can plant, water, and fertilize the seed, but only God can make it grow. Therefore he must wait for the Lord to produce the harvest. When we fast and pray, we are sowing seeds of faith, believing God hears our prayers and will produce a harvest of answers. Therefore you must allow time for the harvest to mature.

On the other hand, your harvest could come quickly because Amos 3:19 says there is a time when reapers will overtake those planting seeds. Sometimes God allows us to go through a process so that we learn obedience and faithfulness to him, and other times he miraculously produces the harvest. We don't know which method God will use to produce the overflow in our lives, but we are confident that it will come.

Although it may take a while to receive the rewards of fasting, the goal is to humble yourself and trust God. When we sincerely humble ourselves and turn away from our sins, God will cause us to overflow in every area of our lives.

Holy Spirit

When you fast and pray in accordance with God's requirements, He also promises to pour out His Spirit upon you. The most significant reward of fasting is receiving God's gift of The Holy Spirit because it means that we are in the right standing with Him and are now empowered to do His will. Joel 2:28-29 says, *"Then, after doing all those things, I will pour out my Spirit upon all people. Your sons and daughters will prophesy. Your old men will dream dreams, and your young men will see visions. In those days, I will pour out my Spirit even on servants—men and women alike."* We know this didn't occur until many years later in Acts 2:2-4 when *"Suddenly, a sound like the blowing of a violent wind came from heaven and filled the whole house where they were sitting. They saw what seemed to be tongues of fire that separated and came to rest on each of them. All of them were filled with the Holy Spirit and began to speak in other tongues as the Spirit enabled them."* Many people did not understand what was happening, so Peter had to explain it to them. He told them, *"These people are not drunk, as you suppose. It's only nine in the morning! No, this is what was spoken by the prophet Joel: 'In the last days, God says, I will pour out my Spirit on all people. Your sons and daughters will prophesy, your young men will see visions, and your old men will dream dreams. Even on my servants, both men and women, I will pour out my Spirit in those days, and they will prophesy."* (Acts 2:15-18). Ironically, the people thought they were drunk, and this was the outpouring of the new wine God promised centuries earlier. He basically told them after I crush you, I will let you ferment for a while, then I will pour out the new wine of my Spirit in you. Observe that the crushing took place over the course of many years. We all want the crushing to end quickly, but we must trust God's process if we want His new wine

Then Peter told them how they could receive the gift of the Holy Spirit. He told them to *"Repent and be baptized, every one of you, in the name of Jesus Christ for the forgiveness of your sins. And you will receive the gift of the Holy Spirit. The promise is for you and your children and for all who are far off—for all whom the Lord our God will call."* Notice that the first thing that Peter told them to do was repent. Fasting is an act of repentance, and that's why it conditions your heart to receive the gift of the Holy Spirit. But you must also ask for the gift Holy Spirit because, like Peter said and Jesus confirmed in Luke 11:13, If you repent from your sins, accept Jesus in your heart, and ask him to baptize you with His Spirit, your heavenly Father will give you the gift of the Holy Spirit.

So as you conclude this fasting study, remember that repentance is the secret to touching the heart of God when you fast. God cares more about building your faith than giving you quick fixes for your problems. God is more interested in your heart than fasting rituals, so repent from any known sins as you fast and ask the Lord to reveal his prophetic instructions for your life and be diligent to obey them.

When you fast, keep in mind all the benefits you can receive through fasting. However, benefits should not be your primary motivation to fast and pray. Your motivation should always be to give God all your heart through fasting and obedience to His will. Your motivation should be to deny your will so that Christ is formed in you.

The Lord will always fulfill His promises and release His prophetic instructions for our lives when we touch His heart through fasting and prayer.

Notes

Briggs, Dean, and Engle, Lou. *The Jesus Fast.* Chosen. Bloomington, MN. 2016.

Franklin, Jentezen. *Fasting.* Charisma House. Lake Mary, Fl. *2008.*

New Living Translation, 2015. Tyndale House Foundation. Biblehub.com.

New International Version. (2011). BibleGateway.com.

Prince, Derek. *Shaping History Through Prayer and Fasting.* Whitaker House. New Kensington, PA. 2001.

Pucket, Susan. *The Science, Methods, and Benefits of Fasting,* https://www.bouldermedicalcenter.com/intermittent-fasting-and-health/.

Seward, William H. "Proclamation Appointing a National Fast Day." *Abraham Lincoln's Proclamation Appointing a National Fast Day,* Roy P. Basler Et al., 30 Mar. 1863, https://www.abrahamlincolnonline.org/lincoln/speeches/fast.htm.

Wallis, Arthur. *God's Chosen Fast.* CLC Publications. Fort Washington, PA. 2001.

About the Author

Charmain Jarrett is the Pastor of Jesus Strong Ministries in Dallas, Texas, which has a global reach via social media. The ministry is a faith-based organization that exists to fulfill the great commission.

Charmain received a life-altering encounter with God while studying to become a medical doctor when the Lord told her, "The lives you will save becoming a medical doctor are nothing compared to the lives that you will save becoming a doctor of My Word."

She then gave up her dream of becoming a medical doctor to follow the call of God. She has earned several college degrees, including a Master's in Theology and a Master's in Business Administration. She is a spirit-filled Bible teacher, pastor, author, songwriter, and entrepreneur.

Pastor Charmain resides in Dallas, Texas, with her husband and Children.

For More Information, Contact

Jesus Strong Ministries
  P.O. Box 9
  Frisco, TX
  75035

You can connect with me on:
- https://jesusstrongministries.org
- https://www.facebook.com/JesusStrongM
- https://www.youtube.com/channel/UCXM5i82IaFNPlEJgZoIPSjw

Also by Charmain Jarrett

We know that we should pray, but most of us don't know how to really pray. When God told Moses to make the tabernacle, its purpose was to be a house of prayer. A meeting place between God and man. This book and help you understand prayer through each dimension of the tabernacle. It will enhance your prayer and teach you how to pray more effectively.

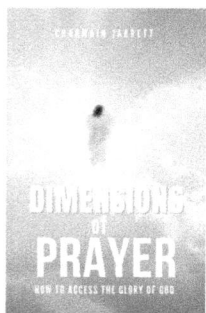

Dimensions of Prayer

God created us to live in glory with him, but sin separates us from his glory. Therefore, he created a pathway to return to his glory, modeled it for us through the Tabernacle in the wilderness, and culminated it with the incarnation of Jesus Christ. This book will teach you how to access God's glory through prayer.